CHAMPIONS OF FREEDOM

The Ludwig von Mises Lecture Series

CHAMPIONS OF FREEDOM

Volume 40

Adam Smith, Free Markets, and the Modern World

Gary Wolfram, Editor

Hillsdale College Press

Hillsdale, Michigan 49242

Hillsdale College Press

CHAMPIONS OF FREEDOM
The Ludwig von Mises Lecture Series—Volume 40
Adam Smith, Free Markets, and the Modern World

©2013 Hillsdale College Press, Hillsdale, Michigan 49242

First printing 2013

The views expressed in this volume are not necessarily the views of Hillsdale College.

Printed in the United States of America

Front cover: The Author of the *Wealth of Nations* by John Kay
©Bettman/Corbis

Library of Congress Control Number: 2001012345

ISBN 978-0-916308-43-8

Contents

Contributors

John Steele Gordon was educated at Millbrook School and Vanderbilt University. Mr. Gordon has been a production editor for Harper & Row (now HarperCollins), and he has served on the staffs of congressmen Herman Badillo and Robert Garcia. His writing has appeared in numerous publications, including *Forbes*, *Forbes ASAP*, *Worth*, *American History*, *National Review*, *Commentary*, *The American*, the *New York Times*, and *The Wall Street Journal*. He is a contributing editor at *American Heritage*, where he wrote the "Business of America" column for many years. He currently writes "The Long View," a column for *Barron's*. He is the author of several books, including *An Empire of Wealth: The Epic History of American Economic Power*.

P. J. O'Rourke received degrees from Miami University in Oxford, Ohio, and Johns Hopkins University. Mr. O'Rourke has served as editor-in-chief of *National Lampoon*, as foreign affairs desk chief at *Rolling Stone*, and as a correspondent for *The Atlantic*. In the fall of 2010, he was the Eugene C. Pulliam Visiting Fellow in Journalism at Hillsdale College. A former board member of Freedom House, he is currently a contributing editor for *The Weekly Standard* and a correspondent for and member of the editorial board of *World Affairs*. In addition, he serves as the Mencken Research Fellow at the Cato Institute and as a board member of the Space Foundation. He is the author of many books, including *On The Wealth of Nations*.

James R. Otteson received his BA from the University of Notre Dame and his AM and PhD from the University of Chicago. He is Joint Professor of Philosophy and Economics and Chairman of Philosophy at Yeshiva University in New York, having taught previously at Georgetown University and the University of Alabama. He is also a senior scholar at the Fund for American Studies in Washington, DC. His books include *Actual Ethics*, which won the 2007 Templeton Enterprise Award, *Adam Smith's Marketplace of Life*, and, most recently, *Adam Smith*. He is currently at work on a book tentatively titled *The End of Socialism*, which will be published by Cambridge University Press in 2013.

Nicholas Phillipson is a graduate of Aberdeen and Cambridge universities and taught history at Edinburgh University. Dr. Phillipson is a research fellow in the School of History, Classics and Archaeology at Edinburgh University. He has held visiting appointments at Princeton University, Yale University, the University of Tulsa, and the Folger Shakespeare Library in Washington, DC. He served as a co-director of a research project on the science of man in Scotland, and was a founding editor of *Modern Intellectual History*. He has written extensively on the history of the Scottish Enlightenment and is the author of *Adam Smith: An Enlightened Life* and *David Hume: The Philosopher as Historian*.

Mark Skousen earned his PhD in monetary economics at George Washington University. Dr. Skousen currently holds the Benjamin Franklin Chair of Management at Grantham University. He has also taught at Columbia Business School, Columbia University, Barnard College, Mercy College, and Rollins College. He is editor-in-chief of *Forecasts & Strategies* and past president of the Foundation for Economic Education. He has written for the *The Wall Street Journal*, *Forbes*, and *The Christian Science Monitor*. He is the author of several books, including *The Making of Modern Economics* (winner of the 2009 Choice Book Award for Outstanding Academic Title) and *The Big Three in Economics: Adam Smith, Karl Marx and John Maynard Keynes*.

Roy C. Smith received his BS from the U.S. Naval Academy and his MBA from Harvard University. Mr. Smith is a Professor of Management Practice and is the Kenneth Langone Professor of Entrepreneurship and Finance at New York University's Leonard N. Stern School of Business. Prior to his current appointment, he was a General Partner of Goldman, Sachs & Co., from which he retired as the senior international partner. In addition to various articles in professional journals and op-ed pieces, he is the author of several books, including *Governing the Modern Corporation* (with Ingo Walter), *Comeback: The Restoration of American Banking Power in the New World Economy*, *The Wealth Creators*, and *Adam Smith and the Origins of American Enterprise*.

Introduction

"Adam Smith, Free Markets, and the Modern World" is an especially appropriate topic for the 2012 Ludwig von Mises Lecture Series. Mises was particularly concerned with how people interact with one another and the type of society that is formed with the interaction of free individuals. The title of his magnum opus, *Human Action*, reflects this.

Developing a theory of human social interaction was also a major concern for Adam Smith, as the authors in this volume point out. *The Theory of Moral Sentiments* and *An Inquiry Into the Nature and Causes of the Wealth of Nations* are Adam Smith's attempts to analyze how people interact with one another and to determine what type of social system will result in the greatest improvement in the standard of living for mankind. Both Smith and Mises came to a similar conclusion—the market system that relies on individual freedom and individual self-interest is the system that will result in what Mises referred to in his book *Liberalism* as wealth creation for the masses.

In his introduction to the 1953 Henry Regnery edition of *An Inquiry Into the Nature and Causes of the Wealth of Nations*, Mises writes about Smith's two volumes:

> Their eminence is to be seen precisely in the fact that they integrated the main body of these ideas into a systematic whole. They presented the essence of the ideology of freedom, individualism, and prosperity, with admirable logical clarity and in an impeccable literary form.[1]

The authors of this volume certainly agree.

Mises went on to comment that reading Smith was particularly important in 1953 because the civilization of freedom and market capitalism that Smith explains was under attack by those who would replace it with central planning. It is now sixty years since Mises wrote this and we find the same conditions and requisite need to read Smith. The massive expansion of the federal government that has been taking place, and the replacement of consumer sovereignty with government intervention in health care, finance, production of power, housing, and a myriad of other arenas makes reading Smith as important today as Mises suggested in 1953.

Nicholas Phillipson brings the insights of a historian to his discussion of Adam Smith. He puts the writings into context by briefly outlining Smith's life history. In particular, Phillipson traces the development of Smith's thought from his studies at Glasgow through his tutoring of the Duke of Buccleuch and the influence of Francis Hutcheson and David Hume.

Phillipson's analysis considers Smith's concern with how the movement to a commercial society would affect the social state, and how governments would react. This was important in Smith's time: As Western Europe evolved from a feudal society to a mercantilist society to a capitalist society, the established social order underwent significant change. It is also very important in today's society as China, India, and other countries move from a centrally planned state toward a market-based system.

P. J. O'Rourke, with his usual ability to get to the heart of the matter, summarizes the *Wealth of Nations* in one sentence: "[T]he key to prosperity is individual self-interest, division of labor, and free trade." The book is so long, O'Rourke contends, because simple ideas are the hardest to get across.

O'Rourke states that the concept that prosperity is a good thing for everyone was foreign to Smith's contemporaries, which is one reason that *Wealth of Nations* was such a path-breaking book. Smith argued that self-interest is a moral good, that division of labor leads to prosperity for all, and that trade should be free from political constraint.

Smith wrote primarily about morals and ethics. O'Rourke maintains that the idea of self-interest could not have been important in a feudal society since most people had little control over what they could accomplish. But the Bible, wherein we learn that we should love our neighbors as ourselves, indirectly says that we can love ourselves.

O'Rourke brings Smith into the current debate over public policy with his view that the price fixing in the massive health care bill will result in shortages, and that some people still find it hard to believe that individual prosperity is good for everyone. Equality under the law is important because we all need others. The market system is what allows us to use the talents of each individual to achieve wealth for all—in spite of the natural frailty of humans.

James Otteson focuses on Smith's first book, the lesser-known *Theory of Moral Sentiments*. He shows how Smith's fundamental assertion that humans have an innate desire for a "mutual sympathy of sentiments" leads to the development of a social order that is much like what Friedrich Hayek (among others) deemed a "spontaneous order." No one is in charge of determining the dress code for presenters at a conference or for what language we use, yet we do not have chaos. All of us desire others to like us, or at least to not find us strange, and so we end up with a sort of marketplace of morality.

Just as no one person determines the price of a good—prices are determined by all of our actions—moral roles are determined by all people, not just one person. Otteson shows that this development of a moral theory is part of a unified theory. *The Theory of Moral Sentiments* formed a single model for all human social interaction connecting economics and morality.

Roy Smith emphasizes Adam Smith's understanding that because the new American colonies did not have an established power structure that could use the political structure to protect the status quo, they had the potential to become one of the most productive societies in the world. He points out that the lessons of Adam Smith were developed most fully in America.

The four primary ideas of Adam Smith's *Wealth of Nations* that Roy Smith develops are free markets, free trade, sound money, and manufacturing. The new colonies successfully adopted these principles and, as a result, America went from a set of nearly empty colonies, barely connected through the Articles of Confederation, to the world's most productive nation.

Mark Skousen examines how central the idea of the invisible hand is to Smith's work. That is, the importance of Smith's contention that individuals acting in their own self-interest will produce benefits for all of society. Skousen points out that Milton Friedman believed Smith's genius was in recognizing that the price system emerging from voluntary exchange allows for the efficient coordination of the activity of millions of individuals. Another Nobel laureate, George Stigler, called the idea of the invisible hand the crown jewel of Smith's writing.

Critiques of laissez-faire claim that, rather than expounding on free markets, Smith was an egalitarian. Skousen notes that mainstream publishers have assigned writers who support big government to write introductions to various editions of the *Wealth of Nations*.

More disturbing for Skousen is that Murray Rothbard, a libertarian economist of the Austrian school, claimed that Smith's contributions are dubious at best and often wrong. This conclusion is in conflict with the writings of Mises who viewed Smith's works as important in demonstrating that the free actions of self-interested individuals result in a free and prosperous society.

After reading Rothbard's criticisms of Smith, Skousen carefully read the *Wealth of Nations* and then *The Theory of Moral Sentiments*. He came to the conclusion that Rothbard was incorrect and Mises and Friedman were right. Smith's general theory of self-interest and his explanation of how humans manage to coordinate activity in a system that is developed rather than invented was a major advance in moral philosophy.

John Steele Gordon examines the advantage that the United States had by being a new country at the time of the Smithian revolution. Smith's ideas could be integrated into society without having to overcome an established power structure. The New World was settled by risk takers, the type of people who become entrepreneurs.

As befits a historian, Gordon points out the significance of events—such as the 1824 Supreme Court case regarding steamship monopolies, the Civil War, and the regulatory effect of the Wagner Act—on the economic development of the United States. Gordon notes that no society prior to the existence of the U.S. had attempted to govern a highly dynamic industrial economy that was a federal republic, and that America's success was due to the insights of the Founders and the writings of Adam Smith.

Adam Smith completed only two books, yet they are among the most significant books ever written. His explanation of why the market system based upon individual liberty and self-interest is both moral and leads to wealth for the masses provided a basis for the economic transformation of the West. Smith's writings are as relevant today as they were in 1776, as the rest of the world moves away from central planning and coercive government toward market capitalism.

Here in America, following the recent election season, it will be useful to keep in mind a final quote from the *Wealth of Nations*:

> The statesman who should attempt to direct private people in what manner they ought to employ their capitals would not only load himself with a most unnecessary attention, but assume an authority which could safely be trusted, not only to no single person, but to no council or senate whatever, and which would nowhere be so dangerous as in the hands of a man who had folly and presumption enough to fancy himself fit to exercise it.[2]

GARY WOLFRAM
William Simon Professor of
Economics and Public Policy
Hillsdale College

Notes

1. Adam Smith, *An Inquiry into the Nature and Causes of the Wealth of Nations: Selections* (Washington, DC: Henry Regnery Co., 1953), introduction. http://mises.org/efandi/ch24.asp.
2. Ibid. (Indianapolis, IN: Liberty Classics, 1981), 456.

Nicholas Phillipson

Adam Smith: Life and Times

The publication of Adam Smith's *Wealth of Nations* on 9th March 1776 was a world-historical event. Whether or not you subscribe to the view that this was one of the most important books ever written, it is certainly one of the handful of texts of the Enlightenment that can be regarded as still alive, as relevant today as it ever was in the lifetime of its author. But the success of the *Wealth of Nations* has had unfortunate and unintended consequences for our understanding of its author. Most of us think of Smith as a one-book man. We forget that he wrote the *Wealth of Nations* as the author of *The Theory of Moral Sentiments*, the remarkable treatise that established him as a moral philosopher of the first rank. Even more of us forget that he spent what he described as "the happiest and most productive years of my life" as a student and later as professor of moral philosophy at Glasgow University, lecturing on rhetoric and jurisprudence as well as ethics, two subjects on which he planned to publish full-length treatises. And virtually no one bothers to read the remarkable unfinished essays on the history of astronomy and aesthetics that were published posthumously. We forget that Smith was a philosopher who promised much and delivered less than he had hoped in terms of publications. It is the job of a historian to try to see Smith in the round, by exploring texts we have forgotten, and asking

1

what light, if any, they shed on the meaning of the great text that forms an essential strand in the intellectual fabric of the postmodern world.

I want to begin with some remarks about documentation, texts, and the problems they give the historian. It is one of the basic facts of Smith's life that he is the worst documented of all the great philosophers of the Enlightenment. He was a notoriously bad correspondent who had to be goaded by his friends into answering letters. To make matters worse, when he was on his deathbed, he destroyed all of his surviving correspondence, all of his lecture notes, and nearly all of his unfinished and unpolished philosophical writings. For while Smith was a reasonably sociable man, he minded about his privacy and, even more, about the prospect of unfinished and unauthorized texts finding their way into print after his death. But what Smith had not counted on was that some of his Glasgow students' lecture notes would eventually turn up. We now have nearly full sets of notes of his lectures on rhetoric and juris-prudence, two of the subjects of those promised full-length treatises that he never delivered. What these notes make clear is that Smith's thinking on these two subjects was highly developed, of great originality, and was indeed ready to be turned into full-length treatises. What is also clear, and what Smith's Scottish friends and students knew, was that Smith had devoted his life to developing a vast and highly integrated account of the principles of human nature, social organization, and history. For this quiet, sociable, and slightly eccentric Scotsman was engaged in the greatest of all of the philosophical projects of the Enlightenment, the development of a Science of Man of which his economic thinking was a part, but only a part. It was a project of Aristotelian proportions, which Smith came within a hairsbreadth of realizing.

Adam Smith was born on 5 June 1723 in Kirkcaldy, a trading port on the east coast of Scotland, a short distance from Edinburgh. His father, an evidently ambitious and well-connected customs official, had died before Smith was born. His mother was the daughter of a reasonably prosperous member of the local gentry. Margaret Smith never remar-ried and devoted the rest of her life to her son. She doted on him, kept house for him for the rest of her long life, and died in 1784, only six years before her son. Smith for his part never married and would come to rely on his mother to provide the privacy, domestic security, and love on which he depended as a philosopher who seems to have driven himself to the edge of a nervous breakdown on more than one occasion. As one of his former pupils once put it, the best routes to Smith's attention were via his philosophy and his mother. To put it bluntly, the budding Aristotle was something of a mother's boy.

Although we know very little about Smith's childhood, what we do know is suggestive. His family and friends were establishment people who supported the Glorious Revolution of 1688, the Presbyterian kirk, and the Act of Union of 1707, the act that was transforming Scotland's economy and its relations with England. They were incomers who had done well out of the new regime, had bought themselves local estates and had set out to improve them. They sent their sons—Smith's friends and contemporaries—to the local school as the first step in preparing them for professional life in a country that seemed to offer new opportunities for national and personal advancement. For Smith it was evidently a happy childhood. His school friends remained friends for the rest of his life and Kirkcaldy was to be his home-base until 1778 when he moved to Edinburgh to become a Commissioner of Customs in Scotland. A belief that a love of improvement was in some sense "natural" to human beings, that it was one of the sources of psychological energy that made civilization and progress possible, was to be fundamental to Smith's science of man. It is very tempting to assume that one of its many taproots lay deep in the soil of Kirkcaldy.

Smith got his philosophical education at Glasgow University between 1736 and 1740, when he was in his teens. Glasgow was a tiny university by modern standards—it had only 13 professors in 1736. But it was a university that had recently gone through a major overhaul, largely dictated by a Whig desire to ensure that its divinity teaching was geared to the business of training moderate Presbyterian ministers and not the radical clergy that had been the cause of so much serious political trouble in the previous century.

Smith was taught exceptionally well. He studied natural philosophy with an evidently thoughtful Newtonian, and developed such an interest in natural science that some of his friends thought that he was heading for a career in that branch of philosophy. Robert Simson, one of the greatest of Enlightenment mathematicians, turned him into a highly competent mathematician; Smith would always value mathematical explanation for its elegance and precision and he would think deeply about its relevance for the human sciences. And most important of all, he was taught moral philosophy by the man he called the "never to be forgotten Francis Hutcheson," an inspiring teacher and the finest moral philosopher in early eighteenth-century Britain. Overall, it was an education that gave him an introduction to the philosophy of the ancient and modern world and an enduring interest in scientific method and the problems of applying it to the study of the human world. It was an admirable education for a budding moral scientist.

Smith owed a lot to Francis Hutcheson. Hutcheson's introductions to the moral philosophy of the ancient and modern world and to the problems of modern philosophy were sophisticated and challenging. And although Smith's philosophical path was to diverge radically from his teacher's, he always acknowledged Hutcheson as one of the architects of the so-called "experimental" approach to the study of human nature. Hutcheson taught Smith to think about the classic questions of moral philosophy—questions about the origins of our ideas of morality, justice, political obligation, natural religion, and beauty—as questions about the meaning of sociability and the problems involved in cultivating it in common life. He rejected classic attempts to show that these ideas were rooted in our natural selfishness or rationality, thinking that these ideas were unproveable and therefore unphilosophical. A genuinely scientific approach to the study of morality ought to begin with empirical questions: How do we become aware of the idea of morality, how do we develop it, and how does it affect our behavior? This meant studying the affections and sentiments that are aroused when we find ourselves ethically challenged by the behavior of others and it meant analyzing the way in which we find ourselves evaluating the conduct of others. Hutcheson thought that experimentation of this sort would show that our conduct was shaped and directed by a moral sense that seemed to be hardwired in some part of our personality and could be cultivated and improved in ways that would turn us into good Christians and good citizens. For example, he was pretty sure that the experience of discovering that we had a moral sense would lead us to think that it must have been installed by a benevolent Creator. As for

politics, Hutcheson's mission was to teach politicians the importance
of understanding the principles of sociability and the problems that
were involved in cultivating it. Such questions had lain at the heart
of the moral and political philosophy of the previous century. Great
philosophers like Grotius, Hobbes, and Pufendorf had reflected on the
disastrous consequences of the sectarian conflicts and civil wars that
had been unleashed by the Reformation and Counter Reformation, and
had threatened to destroy the foundations of political society altogether.
Nearly every European government had been faced with the problem
of rebuilding the foundations of political society and restoring their subjects' capacity for sociability. It was a situation that Hutcheson addressed
in his Glasgow lectures and his lectures raised questions that would lie
at the heart of the *Wealth of Nations*. Smith never forgot Hutcheson's
quasi-sociological approach to the study of morality and sociability,
but he had serious reservations about it. Was it really plausible to think
of our social behavior as being regulated by a moral sense no one had
ever noticed before? Was it plausible to think of a sense of morality as
the foundation stone on which our capacity for sociability was based?
What about the sense of fairness and justice? And, most seriously of
all, wasn't Hutcheson introducing theology by the back door by hinting
that this curious moral sense had been installed in us by the deity? All
of Smith's understanding of the principles of human nature worked
on the assumption that the moral sensibility we acquire in the course
of ordinary life has its roots in social education and everyday experience. It meant taking an essentially non-Christian, socio-psychological
approach to a subject that had always been impregnated with theological
assumptions. I am certain that Smith laid the foundations of his own
approach to the science of man between 1740 and 1746 when he was
in his late teens and early twenties and a student at Oxford. He may
have hated the university and rubbished it memorably in the *Wealth of
Nations*, but it provided him with six years of private study. And it was
almost certainly in the course of this private study that he encountered
the philosophy of the man who was to become his greatest friend and
the greatest influence on his philosophy, David Hume.

Hume's masterpiece, the *Treatise of Human Nature*, was published
in 1739–40. It was a profoundly skeptical work. Hume demonstrated
decisively that it was impossible to show that reason has the power to

regulate our understanding of the world unless one makes the deeply unphilosophical assumption that it had been cognitively supercharged by the deity with special unobservable powers. Hume concluded that all of our thinking about the world, about ourselves, and about our duties to others had its roots in the imagination, the passions, and the cognitive customs and habits we acquire in the course of common life. This skeptical philosophy pointed toward a theory of sociability that Smith was to adopt in its entirely. Hume thought that the rock on which our capacity for sociability is built is the sense of fairness and justice we acquire from a very early age in competing for scarce resources and learning the meaning of "property." He thought that our willingness to submit to political authority had its roots in the belief that it is on this that the security of our persons and property depends. He thought that our ability to function as genuinely sociable agents is only possible when we feel secure enough to regularize our relations with others. Hume's insights pointed to a new approach to the science of man that would involve exploring the anatomy of the moral sensibility we develop in the course of common life. It was an approach that emphasized the *historicity* of human nature and the importance of understanding the *processes* by which we come to know the world. As Hume knew very well, that would involve studying the way in which our personalities were formed in the political societies and civilizations in which we are born, raised, and lived our lives.

But it is important to think of Smith as a critic as well as a disciple of Hume. For example, while Hume had written brilliantly about the *processes* by which our sentiments and understanding are formed and clearly knew that language and conversation had an all-important part to play in the process, he had conspicuously failed to produce a developed theory of language. In the same way, when discussing the origins of our sense of justice, and pinpointing the importance of property in shaping that sense, he had failed to ask the historical question—how that sense of justice would differ in different types of property-owning societies. And beyond that, while it was clear that Hume's entire philosophy rested on the assumption that all human behavior is somehow driven by *need*, he had, once again, failed to develop an appropriate *theory* that took account of the fact that need means different things in different types of society. In other words, although Hume had laid the *foundations* of a revolutionary science of man, he had failed to develop the explanatory *system* from which general laws about human behavior could be deduced. Developing that system and showing how it could be used to educate modern citizens and governments about their natures and duties was to be Smith's driving intellectual ambition for the rest of his life.

Smith laid down the fundamentals of his system between 1748 and 1762 in lectures and papers he gave in Edinburgh in 1748–50 and developed in Glasgow as professor of moral philosophy from 1752–63. Taken together they added up to an analysis of the different strands of the sensibility that a sociable agent needs to acquire if he is to survive and prosper in civil society. The lectures on rhetoric dealt with the sense of propriety we acquire in developing the language skills on which all social life depends. The lectures on morals he gave in Glasgow and published in 1759 as *The Theory of Moral Sentiments* dealt with the origin of the senses of morality, justice, and political obligation on which our capacity for sociability depended. In the lectures on jurisprudence he discussed the way in which our sense of fairness and justice varied in different types of property-owning societies with different types of government, and he paid particular attention to the role of governments in preserving and refining our understanding of justice. It is important to note that it was in this context that Smith set out his first thoughts on political economy and the problem of preserving the rules of justice in a commercial age. His fragmentary papers on the history of philosophy and on aesthetics were designed to show that the credibility of any system of art and philosophy will ultimately depend upon their appeal to the sense of beauty and truthfulness of the public at any particular moment in time. Smith was, in other words, developing a sentimental, historized science of man that not only explored what we would call the process of socialization, but also showed how we acquire a sense of identity and individuality. But what underpinned this immensely powerful system was a sophisticated theory of need, first suggested at the start of the lectures on rhetoric, subsequently developed in the lectures on jurisprudence, and latterly used to underpin the *Wealth of Nations*: It is a theory based on a conjecture about sociability derived from Bernard Mandeville's *Fable of the Bees*.

Like Mandeville, Smith began by asking what distinguishes man from the other animals. It had nothing to do with man's supposed rationality or his equally supposititious possession of a Hutchesonian moral sense. Man differed from the brutes simply by virtue of his physical frailty. Aboriginal man, living in a world of wild beasts and natural hardship, had learnt the hard way that to survive he had to cooperate; that cooperation meant exchanging ideas, sentiments, services; that some form of communication, some form of language was necessary to make cooperation possible. Society was thus a response to need, and sociability was a matter of communication and trust. Accounting for progress and social change in any particular society would therefore be a matter of explaining changes in its pattern of need.

Smith's thoughts on the causes of the multiplication of needs were at the heart of his theory. He began by asking under what conditions a society's needs would multiply. His answer took the form of a characteristically unobtrusive but sweeping conjecture: Human beings seem to be endowed with a natural love of improvement and will exercise it when they feel secure enough to do so. For Smith, improvement was a matter of seeking to make one's life more "convenient" whenever one had the opportunity to do so. Thus members of primitive societies will exchange caves for huts, clothes for nakedness, cooked meat for raw, and so on, whenever security and technology make it possible for them to do so. But this taste for improvement will have further unintended consequences as new circumstances start to press on our sense of fairness, entitlement, and justice and on our expectations of government. As Smith commented:

> The whole industry of human life is employed not in procuring the supply of our three humble necessities, food, cloaths, and lodging, but in procuring the conveniences of it according to the delicacy of our taste. To improve and multiply the materials which are the principal objects of our necessities, gives occasion to all the variety of the arts.[1]

Smith's theory of need had taken the form of a powerful conjectural history of civilization as it progresses from its savage to its pastoral, feudal, and commercial states, and it was to be elaborated and refined in every aspect of his work; in fact, it is his most enduring contribution to the modern understanding of history. In the lectures of jurisprudence, he developed complementary and interlocking conjectural histories of property and government that were illustrated with examples drawn from real history and used as a benchmark against which to raise fascinating and often brilliant discussions about the experience of societies whose histories did not conform to these conjectural norms. In his fragmentary writings about aesthetics and philosophy, he was to apply the model to the history of taste and science. Most famously, in the *Wealth of Nations*, he was to develop an astonishingly daring and controversial conjectural account of the "natural" progress of commerce in Europe in order to raise the deeply conjectural, and some would say unhistorical question, Why had the progress of commerce been so slow in Europe? But unhistorical or not, it was a conjecture on which much of the argumentation about the workings of the market and the role of governments in regulating them was to be based. All of this thinking was in place by 1763 when Smith resigned from his post as professor of moral philosophy at Glasgow, took up the strikingly well-paid post of tutor to the young Duke of Bucclecuch, travelled to France with his new pupil, and began work on the text of the *Wealth of Nations*, a task he would complete thirteen years later.

Smith had come to political economy with a theory of human nature that held that all human life can be seen as life is a matter of exchange and that exchanging goods, services, and sentiments is "natural" to humankind, in the sense that it is dictated by need. It was a theory that argued that it is from the experience of learning to live in society that we acquire a sense of what fairness, justice, political obligation, and morality mean, even though some of us act from time to time in ways that we know are unfair, unjust, treasonable, or immoral. After all, those who would say they believe that greed is good know perfectly well that most of us do not believe it. But over and above that, Smith's theory had shown that social experience and moral education of this kind provides us with a sense of individuality and identity. For the notion that individualism is a product of sociability is one of the deepest paradoxes of Smith's Science of Man.

Smith had also shown that the seeds of progress are rooted in human nature and in that apparently "natural" love of improvement that is characteristic of our species, and that will flourish when we feel secure. His lectures on government had explored the problems experienced by governments in different countries and civilizations in enforcing the rules of justice on which our sense of security is founded and, like Hume, he was in no doubt of the difficulties all rulers face in performing this primary task. His unique contribution to the theory of government was to address the complex problems that governments face when their economies are in a state of transition, as pastoral societies morph into feudal and as feudal societies morph into commercial. It was to be a problem of central importance to him in writing the *Wealth of Nations*.

The *Wealth of Nations* is about the problems of managing the political affairs of a postfeudal civilization that was being transformed by the pressures of the market on its land, labor, and capital resources, and by the effects of war, empire, and globalization on society and government in different countries and civilizations. Smith was particularly interested in the effects of commercial expansion on the class system of his own country, and on the wealth, culture, expectations of government, and, above all, on the sense of interest of different classes. Some of these classes had privileged access to government; others, none at all. Some were ruthlessly exploitative and opportunistic in advancing their interests. Each class had its own philosophies and superstitions and expectations of government. And each, in different ways, was discovering that their expectations and sense of entitlement were being challenged by the progress of commercialization and the market.

As a conjectural historian, and as a brilliant theorist of the market, Smith had no doubts about the civilizing and liberalizing tendencies of commerce. But what readers of the *Wealth of Nations* often forget is that, historically speaking, its cutting edge is an extended discussion of the problems governments faced in managing the process of liberalization. At one level, Smith's purpose was to provide a persuasive account of the natural progress of commerce in a relatively secure world that emphasized the long-term benefits that commerce and the liberalization of the market would bring to rich, poor, and the nation at large. But half of the *Wealth of Nations* was devoted to the problems governments face in managing such changes. Smith was acutely aware that the process of liberalization would inevitably challenge established ideas of fairness and natural justice, and he was well aware of the lengths to which different classes could and would go to defend them. What is more, he was in no doubt that badly handled by incompetent or ignorant rulers, the process of liberalization would weaken and even threaten the very sociability on which the survival of society depended.

Seen in this context some of the great themes of the *Wealth of Nations* concern the dilemmas governments face when attempting to square the long-term good that liberalization brings with the short-term problems involved in maintaining the sociability on which political stability and future long-term progress depends. In addressing this dilemma, Smith was no utopian. As he wrote, "To expect indeed that the freedom of trade should ever be entirely restored in Great Britain is as absurd as to expect an Oceana or Utopia should be established in it."[2] For in the last resort, in addressing the tension that will always exist between the long-term demands of liberalization and the shorter-term demands of maintaining sociability, Smith would always remain the spokesman of the spirit of a carefully judged pragmatism. It is the spirit of the natural jurisprudence to which he had been introduced by Francis Hutcheson, the spirit of that gradualist faith in the power of improvement to which he was so deeply committed. It is also the spirit of a philosopher of the Enlightenment.

Notes

1. Adam Smith, *Lectures on Jurisprudence* [1762], edited by R. L. Meek, D. D. Raphael, and P. G. Stein (Indianapolis, IN: Liberty Fund, 1982), 488–89.
2. Adam Smith, *An Inquiry into the Nature and Causes of the Wealth of Nations* [1776], edited by R. H. Campbell and A. S. Skinner (Indianapolis, IN: Liberty Classics, 1981), 471.

P. J. O'ROURKE

A Book that Changed the World

The *Wealth of Nations* is a very long book, and yet it is a very simple book. It is so simple that it can be summed up in one sentence: The key to prosperity is individual self-interest, division of labor, and free trade.

The *Wealth of Nations* is very long because it is very simple. The simplest points are the hardest to get across. Anybody who has raised a teenager knows this. How many millions of words—enough to fill the *Wealth of Nations* ten times over—have been used by every father of every teenage boy to say, "Turn your hat around, pull your pants up, and get a job"?

And so it was with Adam Smith, speaking to an eighteenth-century world that was as ignorant of economics as any unemployed teen living at home in his parents' basement.

Smith had a great ethical revelation to announce: Prosperity is a good thing for everybody to have. From this revelation he derived three logical points: A moral point—that self-interest is not immoral; a practical point—that division of labor must be practiced; and a political point—that trade should be free from political constraint.

Smith's great ethical revelation doesn't sound so great to us. That "prosperity is a good thing for everybody to have" seems painfully obvious. Who could disagree? Newt Gingrich and Nancy Pelosi are dancing cheek-to-cheek to that tune.

But this wasn't always the case. Once upon a time, the nobility thought that if the commoners became prosperous they could get uppity, and who knew what would happen? Some cute girl whose family made a fortune in mail-order party favors might marry the future king of England. The middle classes thought that if the lower classes became prosperous it could lead to loud music, vulgar language, and people with tattoos having their own reality TV shows.

If you read the eighteenth-century novels of Tobias Smollet— Adam Smith's nearly exact contemporary—you will see these views on bold display. In *The Expedition of Humphrey Clinker*, published five years before the *Wealth of Nations*, the protagonist is a wealthy country gentleman named Matthew Bramble. Bramble is portrayed as upright, admirable, exceedingly kind-hearted and charitable, and filled to the brim with common sense. He is one of those fictional characters who make fiction into fiction by being too good to be true. But listen to the estimable Matthew Bramble, Esquire, on the subject of economically thriving eighteenth-century London, where all sorts of "everybodies" are getting prosperous:

> The gayest places of public entertainment are filled with fashionable figures; which, upon inquiry, will be found to be journeymen tailors, serving-men, and ladies' maids, disguised like their betters.[1]

Bramble, so supposedly full of common sense, is also full of spleen about this general prosperity, and, to modern ears, full of b.s., too:

> "There is no distinction or subordination left," Bramble sputters. He says, "The different departments of life are jumbled together—the hod-carrier, the low mechanic, the tapster, the publican, the shop-keeper, the pettifogger, the citizen…[all] actuated by the demons of profligacy."[2]

"Profligacy"—ordinary people having too much money. How disgusting. Smollet, through Bramble, says there are many sources of this lack of "distinction" and "subordination" that alarm him so much. But, he says, "They may all be resolved into the grand source of luxury."

"Luxury"—ordinary people having too much money. Prosperity is *not*, as far as Smollet is concerned, a good thing for everybody to have.

Now, Smollet was a decent man. From what we can tell he was almost as kind-hearted and charitable as his hero Matthew Bramble. And we know from Smollet's novels that he was keenly aware of, and detested, the social and economic injustice of his times.

Smollet was also an educated man. He attended Glasgow University at the same time as Adam Smith, and they seem to have been acquainted. Smith is mentioned, in passing, in *Humphrey Clinker*. Smollet was familiar with all the great thinkers of eighteenth-century Britain and was a prominent literary figure in his own right.

Therefore, when we see a man like Tobias Smollet saying that poor people have too much money, we can be pretty sure that what we are seeing is what right-thinking people of the time thought. We are in the presence of "received wisdom." We are reading a *New York Times* editorial, listening to an NPR commentary, hearing President Obama give a campaign speech.

We are not the first to live in an era when right-thinking people don't know what the hell they are talking about.

Opinions like Smollet's caused a rare—in fact, I think, the only—outburst of sarcasm in the *Wealth of Nations*. In the chapter on "The Wages of Labor," an obviously furious Smith asks, "Is this improvement in the circumstances of the lower ranks of the people to be regarded as an advantage or as an *inconveniency* to the society?"[3]

Poor people having the material means to do what they want: It would be so *inconvenient*! They might want to dine in nice restaurants. They might want to live in your neighborhood. They might want their children to go to private schools. They might want to vote for people they approve of instead of people the political machines tell them to vote for.

We could pause here for a moment and ask ourselves whether this attitude of "inconveniency" isn't at the heart of a lot of America's "poverty programs"—food stamps, public housing, No Child Left Behind....

But at least everyone in America today, left and right, from Sarah Palin to Harry Reid, pays lip service to the idea that "prosperity is a good thing for everybody to have."

So why, in Adam Smith's time, was prosperity not considered a self-evident benefit for "the lower ranks of the people"? Because nobody had bothered to *ask* them! In many places around the world—including our own inner cities—nobody has bothered to ask them yet.

Everybody thinks the *Wealth of Nations* is a book about economics, and, of course, it is. Adam Smith invented modern economics. (Whether we should thank him for that is between you and your financial advisor.)

But an economics book—however brilliant—is just a way to understand and analyze the goods and services provided by people. People are going to continue to provide these goods and services whether there is a book about it or not.

The even greater importance of the *Wealth of Nations* is that it is a book about ethics and morals. In fact, Smith was first and foremost a moral philosopher. He spent the better part of his career writing and revising what he considered to be his more important book, *The Theory of Moral Sentiments*. And, if the *Wealth of Nations* isn't long enough for you, I suggest reading *The Theory of Moral Sentiments*, too—a brilliant book about how the innate tendency of humans to be sympathetic develops into the not-so-innate tendency of humans to be moral. I would call the philosophical design that Adam Smith draws in *Moral Sentiments* nothing less than the mechanical engineering of the Holy Ghost. So Smith takes up economics with a full understanding of its moral implications.

Actually, a lot of people used to have this understanding. Cambridge University did not separate the study of economics from the study of moral sciences until 1903—a little soon.

Armed with the ethical revelation that prosperity is a good thing for everybody to have, and knowing that there is no philosophical or God-given reason to think otherwise, Smith sets out to demystify economics, to take the *meta* out of the *metaphysics*. And he does so in one astonishing sentence that should be etched into the bifocal lenses of every economist in the world: "Consumption is the sole end and purpose of all production."[4]

Economics is our livelihood, and just that.

In order to better that livelihood, Smith argues three basic principles, and, by plain thinking and plentiful examples (maybe *too* plentiful, given that *Wealth of Nations* is a thousand pages long), he proves them. Even intellectuals should have no trouble understanding Smith's ideas.

Prosperity depends upon the trinity of individual prerogatives—pursuit of self-interest, division of labor, and freedom of trade.

Smith's first principle—and his vital contribution to the morality of economics—is that there is nothing inherently wrong with a person pursuing his own self-interest. As with the universal benefit of prosperity, this doesn't sound like news to us. Or rather, pursuit of self-interest sounds like everything in the news. We assume everyone is pursuing his own self-interest, and, to the extent it doesn't interfere with our self-interest, we approve. These days, altruism itself has a publicist. It is in a person's self-interest to be a celebrity. Bono has figured out a way to stay one.

But it didn't used to be like that. Social elites, politicians, philosophers, and religious leaders used to tell everybody to suck it up—subjugate your ego, bridle your ambitions, sacrifice yourself to God, to Stoicism, to the feudal big shots. We bought it because we didn't have any control over our self-interest anyway. If we were slaves or serfs—and most of us were—we didn't even have a proper self to be self-interested in. In the doghouse of ancient and medieval existence, asceticism made us feel less like dogs.

But by Adam Smith's time in eighteenth-century Britain, ordinary people were beginning to have some control over their own destinies. This, per our example from Smollet, did not please a lot of social elites, politicians, philosophers, or religious leaders (or popular novelists).

However, Smith understood the logic of scripture. When God speaks to Moses—Leviticus 19:18—and says, "thou shalt love thy neighbor as thyself," God is signing off on it being okay for us to love ourselves and to have a self-interest. Smith was pointing out that it is never a question of social vulgarity, political treason, philosophical folly, or religious sacrilege to better our material circumstances. The question is how to do it.

The answer was Smith's second principle: division of labor—what we would call "specialization." No one before Adam Smith seemed to have realized how important the division of labor is to economic progress. Indeed, Adam Smith invented the term.

Of course division of labor has been around since caveman times. The wily fellow with the big ideas chips the spear points. The courageous oaf spears the mammoth. The artistic type does a lovely cave painting of it all. This leads inexorably to trade. One person makes a thing. Another person makes another thing. And everybody wants everything.

Hence, Adam Smith's third principle—free trade. All trades, when freely conducted, are mutually beneficial by definition.

That doesn't mean there are no stupid trades. A cave painting may not be worth 300 pounds of mammoth ham. A starving cave artist gorges himself for months while a new art patron stands scratching his head in the Paleolithic grotto. And what about that wily spear point-chipper? He doubtless took his mammoth cut. But these participants in free trade didn't ask us. It's none of our business.

Unless, of course, we make it our business by introducing trade regulation. A regulation can't be effective without coercion to enforce it. So, suddenly, instead of free trade, we have coercive trade: I get the spear points, and the mammoth meat, and the cave painting, and the cave. And what you get is killed.

Coercion is, very simply, the lack of individual liberty. Coercion destroys the mutually beneficial nature of trade, which destroys the trading, which destroys the division of labor, which destroys progress. You can have pursuit of self-interest, division of labor, and freedom of trade. Or you can have the old Soviet Union.

You see, not only was Adam Smith an important ethicist and an important moralist, he was also an important defender of liberty. His defense of liberty in the *Wealth of Nations* goes well beyond his defense of equal economic opportunities and the individual prerogatives entailed in bettering one's own condition—having labor rights and being allowed to exchange goods and services.

By showing how productivity is increased Smith disproved the idea that bettering the condition of one person necessarily worsens the condition of somebody else—an idea still dearly held by Marxists. And everybody's little brother.

Wealth is not a pizza where if I have too many slices you have to eat the Domino's box. Wealth is not zero sum.

Our politicians should get this through their head. They keeps harping on how there is a huge income disparity between the very rich and ordinary Americans and how we have to close that gap because it is so unfair.

Well, Adam Smith is here to speak in favor of unfairness. I do the same at home. My eleven-year-old daughter is always saying, "That's not fair." And I say, "You're cute. That's not fair. Your family's pretty well-off. That's not fair. You were born in America. *That's* not fair. You'd better get down on your knees and pray to God that things don't start getting 'fair' for you."

To heck with the income disparity gap. What we need is more income, even if it means a bigger gap.

Adam Smith freed us from the ideology of redistribution and all the totalitarian powers such an ideology requires. Adam Smith also freed us from the mercantilist theory and all the bureaucratic powers that theory requires to ensure a "balance of trade."

Smith showed that there is no such thing as a "trade imbalance," such as the "trade imbalance" we supposedly have with China. All trades are balanced the moment they are completed. That is the definition of a "trade."

Back in the 1980s everyone was panicked about the "trade imbalance" with Japan. Japan was sending us all these cars and stereos and TVs, and all they were getting in return were little green pieces of paper with pictures of dead presidents on them—which they didn't know what to do with. They didn't want anything America was making at the time, except Michael Jackson tape cassettes. (And we weren't even making the valuable part—the cassette.) So the Japanese decided to buy America itself. They bought Pebble Beach. They bought Rockefeller Center. And everyone was freaking out—as if the Japanese were going to take Pebble Beach home or something.

The Japanese kept buying commercial real estate until there was a huge bubble. And then the bubble did what bubbles do. As a result, at the end of the 1980s, America had all the cars and stereos and TVs and Pebble Beach and Rockefeller Center *and* all those little green pieces of paper, too. The Japanese had stuck their economy where the rising sun never shines.

So if American politicians insist on worrying about our current "trade imbalance" with China, what they should worry about is what it will do to the Chinese.

There are a lot of lessons in the *Wealth of Nations* that America's politicians from both parties should study before they set out to curtail our liberty by taking our economic freedoms.

It is to Smith that we owe the understanding that an attempt to use the law to fix prices below market value causes the good or the service that has had its price fixed to disappear from that market.

What is President Obama's health care bill except price fixing? The price fixing that works so well in Cuba and North Korea. And in New York City's rent-controlled apartments. Everybody knows how easy it is to find an inexpensive apartment in a nice neighborhood in New York.

Fixed prices in a health care system ultimately run by the government will drive the best people out of the business. Who wants to spend a quarter of his lifetime studying to be a doctor just to become a government bureaucratic hack?

Someday we will be wheeled in for a heart bypass operation and the surgeon will be the same person who is now behind the counter when we renew our car registration at the Department of Motor Vehicles.

If we are not careful, what we will wind up with is a health care system like they have in Canada, a nation that has been nearly beggared by health care spending—even though Canada is a sparsely populated country with a shortage of gunshot wounds, crack addicts, and huge tort judgments.

And, anyway, what are Americans supposed to gain from a Canadian-style health care system devoted to hockey injuries and sinus infections caused by trying to pronounce French vowels?

We had better listen to Adam Smith before it is too late. In fact, we had better listen to Adam Smith in any case. Smith was a defender of material freedom. He was a defender of political freedom. But most of all he was a defender of mental freedom.

He freed our minds from a number of bad ideas about money. It is this freedom, as much as our other freedoms, that has allowed our modern economy with it widespread prosperity to flourish.

By showing that there is no set amount of wealth Smith disproved the idea that a nation has a certain fixed horde of treasure—a king's ransom, as it were, of gold, silver, and jewels. No, said Smith, the wealth of a nation has to be measured by its volume of trades in goods and services—by what goes on in the royal castle's kitchens and stables, not by what is locked in the royal vaults.

In other words, it was Smith who invented the concept of gross domestic product, GDP. (And without GDP modern economists would have nothing to say. They'd be standing around mute in ugly neckties, waiting for the Bloomberg Network to ask them to be silent on the air.)

If wealth is all ebb and flow, then so is its measure, money. Money has no intrinsic value. Any baby who has swallowed a nickel could tell you so. Those of us old enough to have heard about the German Weimar Republic and to have lived through the Jimmy Carter administration are not pained by this information. But in the eighteenth century money was still precious metals. What Smith had to say about money bothered his contemporaries. He said that gold is, well, definitely worth its weight in gold—but not so definitely worth anything else. People were upset by this—even though they could see that eighteenth-century Spain was covered with bling and completely impoverished, so Smith was obviously right. But it was as if Smith, who had just proved that everybody could have more money, then proved that money didn't buy happiness. And it doesn't. It rents it.

What Smith had to say in the *Wealth of Nations* disturbed people at a visceral level. It still does. It disturbs me. And I'm a free market libertarian Republican, a capitalist pig—not, perhaps, a member of the 1 percent, but not for lack of trying. I am reading Smith about how pursuit of self-interest is a good thing, yet still somewhere in the back of my mind I'm thinking, "Gee, *I'm* not self-interested, *I'm* not selfish, *I'm* not greedy. I care about the environment. And I want to elect people who care about the environment the way I do. Because if we elect a bunch of environmentalists then that subdivision full of McMansions that's going to block my view of the ocean won't get built."

And I'm thinking, "Let's face it, the 'lower ranks for the people' *do* have too much money. Look at those Kardashian sisters. Or those Wall Street types buying the chateaux-to-go on my beachfront. Them with their four-barge garage and the Martha Stewart kitchen that they cook in about as often as Martha does the dishes. They may think they're not the 'lower ranks' because they've got a lot of dough, but their lifestyle is an 'inconveniency to the society' big time, as they'll find out when I key their Hummer that's taking up three parking spaces."

I catch myself drifting away from the Adam Smith admiration of pursuit of self-interest, division of labor, and freedom of trade.

I say to myself, "These self-interested types, all they do is work all day. Eighty or 100 hours a week, in some specialized division of labor that nobody understands—in bailed-out investment banks or fancy corporate law firms or expensive hospital operating rooms. They shouldn't be free to trade their money for anything they want, they should give it to me."

Mentally, I rebel against busting my hump in a specialized job and getting everything I need through commerce with other people. Which is why my wife and I are planning to grow all our own food (turnips can be stored for a year!), use only fair-traded internet services with open-code programming, heat the house by means of clean energy renewable resources (such as wind power from the draft under the front door), and knit our children's' clothes with organic wool from sheep raised under humane farming conditions in our yard. This will keep the kids warm and cozy, if somewhat itchy, and will build their characters because they will get teased on the street.

Okay, sure, total removal of all trade restrictions would be "good for the economy." But think of the danger and damage to society. If it weren't for government regulation of markets, investment funds like MF Global could have cheated investors out of millions. Without government restrictions on the sale of hazardous substances, young people might smoke, drink, even use drugs. If we didn't have the trade restraints of labor unions thousands of poor souls would still be wage slaves in the rust belt, their daily lives filled with mindless drudgery. And if it weren't for OPEC monopoly controls filling stations could charge as little as they like. I would have to drive all over town to find the best price, and that would waste energy and release greenhouse gases. So we have to have regulation.

Consider the harm free trade does to the developing world. Cheap pop music iTune downloads from the U.S. will put every nose flute band in Peru out of business.

Plus some jobs require protection, to ensure that they are performed locally, in their own communities. My job is to make quips, jests, and waggish comments. Somewhere in Mumbai there is a younger, funnier person willing to work for less. My job could be outsourced to him. But Mumbai-Me is thousands of miles away. He could make any joke he wanted without thought of the consequences. He could let his sense of humor run wild and make jokes about Ron Paul—how he's so libertarian that if he were elected you'd not only *get* to do anything you wanted, you'd *have* to do anything you wanted. A half-gallon of ice cream and a pack of Marlboros for lunch. But, then, who would my fellow libertarians be offended by? Who would my wife scold for rudeness? Who would my friends shun?

Plus there is all that *Wealth of Nations* ebb and flow of goods and services—Smith's gross domestic product. I am as grossly domestic as the next person. Where is the product? How come all the goods and services ebb out of my income instead of flow into it? Of course I understand that money isn't what is intrinsically valuable. Love is what is intrinsically valuable. And my bank account is full of love. In the tennis score sense of the word.

You see, 236 years after the *Wealth of Nations* was published it is still very hard for us to understand and believe in what Adam Smith had to say.

But it is important to understand the *Wealth of Nations*—not just so that we can understand economics, but so that we can understand the moral lesson that Adam Smith was trying to convey. The moral lesson is the necessity of freedom and equality.

The *Wealth of Nations* concerns itself with economics because freedom and equality are so morally necessary that without them we cannot even perform the humble but morally necessary tasks of feeding, clothing, and sheltering those whom we love.

The *Wealth of Nations* espouses free enterprise not because free enterprise will make us rich—though we hope it will—but because free enterprise is based upon property rights. The property rights that are important are not those that Donald Trump has but those that we all have—the deeds to ourselves, our self-possession as free individuals.

Adam Smith said, "The property which every man has in his own labor, as it is the original foundation of all other property, so it is the most sacred."[5] Smith said that no matter how poor we are, we all have a fortune and an estate and an investment portfolio in "the strength and dexterity of our hands." It is from this humble grasp of—call it a hammer and a sickle—that all free enterprise comes.

Smith said that to hinder a person from employing strength and dexterity in whatever manner that person thinks proper—without injury to his neighbor—is a violation of the most sacred property. I call it me. You call it you.

Furthermore, this property of freedom is meaningless unless we are all created equal. As a well-known document published the same year as the *Wealth of Nations* puts it: "We hold that truth to be self-evident." But why? Are we all equal because we all showed up? It doesn't work that way at weddings and funerals. Are we all equal because it says so in the United Nation's Universal Declaration of Human Rights? The UN also says "Everyone has the right to rest and leisure, including reasonable limitation of working hours." I'll have my wife tell the kids.

No, it was Adam Smith, writing about mere economics who explained why we are all equal. It is because man, the most powerful creature ever to bestride the earth, is also the most pitifully helpless. We are born incapable of caring for ourselves and remain so—to judge by today's youth—until we are about 40. At the age of two when any other mammal is in its peak earning years, the human toddler cannot find its behind with both hands—at least not well enough to use the potty. The whole creativity of a Daniel Defoe couldn't get Robinson Crusoe through the workweek without a supply of manufactured goods from the shipwreck and the services of a cannibal executive assistant.

We must treat other people with the respect due to equals not because we are inspired with noble principle or filled with fraternal affection but because we are pathetic and useless. I quote Adam Smith: "An individual stands at all times in need of the cooperation and assistance of great multitudes, while his whole life is scarce sufficient to gain the friendship of a few persons."[6]

Think about that. On the face of it, it is a remarkably left-wing statement, almost a heartfelt plea for socialism. And yet that very sentence is the prologue to the single most-quoted passage in the *Wealth of Nations*: "It is not from the benevolence of the butcher, the brewer, or the baker, that we expect our dinner, but from their regard to their own self-interest."

And *this* is always quoted as if it meant "greed is good."

That is not the meaning of the *Wealth of Nations*. Adam Smith does not urge us to selfishly pursue wealth in the free enterprise system. He urges us to give thanks that the butcher, the brewer, and the baker do.

The butcher, the brewer, and the baker may be wonderful people. Or they may be greedy swine. That is not the point. The point that Adam Smith is making is that the butcher, the brewer, and the baker are endowed by their creator with certain unalienable rights and among these are steak, beer, and hoagie rolls.

Notes

1. Tobias Smollet, *The Expedition of Humprhy Clinker* [1771] (Oxford, UK: Oxford University Press, 2006), 88.
2. Ibid.
3. Adam Smith, *An Inquiry into the Nature and Causes of the Wealth of Nations* [1776], edited by R. H. Campbell and A. S. Skinner (Indianapolis, IN: Liberty Classics, 1981), 36.
4. Ibid., 660.
5. Ibid., 138.
6. Ibid., 26–27.

JAMES OTTESON

Smith's Other Book:
The Theory of Moral Sentiments

Adam Smith was a professor of moral philosophy at the University of Glasgow. In addition to the *Wealth of Nations*, he wrote a book entitled *The Theory of Moral Sentiments*. In the eighteenth century, professors were divided between two large categories. If you studied what we might now think of as the sciences, in particular the hard sciences, you were a professor of natural philosophy; if you studied anything regarding human beings or human behavior—which would include many of the now-separate disciplines of history, literature, anthropology, economics—you were a professor of moral philosophy. As someone whose training is in philosophy, I take great pleasure in the idea that all professors in the eighteenth century were called philosophers whether they were studying the natural world or the human world.

Adam Smith was one of the luminaries of an astonishing period of learning called the Scottish Enlightenment, a period that roughly paralleled his lifetime. That wasn't the term that the eighteenth-century Scots used, although there was a sense, even then, that something special was going on. Scotland seems a rather unusual and unlikely place to have been at the forefront of nearly every single intellectual endeavor in human study, but it surely was. In nearly every discipline—mathematics, medicine, geology, and, of course, economics—nearly all of the leading lights of the time were in Scotland.

Adam Smith published only two books in his life. We do have students' notes from his lectures on jurisprudence, and work he did on lectures on rhetoric, and some *belles lettres*. We also have a handful of his essays. But he wrote only two books. The first, *The Theory of Moral Sentiments*, was published in 1759. It is basically a stitching-together of his lecture notes into a single comprehensive argument. The second book is the *Wealth of Nations*, which was published in 1776—an auspicious year, and also the year in which David Hume died.

In *The Theory of Moral Sentiments*, he examined the origins and nature of human morality. One thing to note immediately is that the book was uncharacteristically free—though not entirely—of what we might think of as moralizing. You won't find many instances of Smith saying "here's how you ought to behave to be moral and here's how you ought not to behave to be moral." What he does in the book is try to understand, as a social scientist might, what this phenomenon of human moral judgment-making is all about. How is it that human beings come to have the moral views they do? How can we explain various aspects of the observable phenomena of human moral judgment-making? He also talks about something he calls "sympathy," which I will discuss later. It plays a very important role in the mechanism that he is to develop.

In the *Wealth of Nations*, Smith examines economic issues—markets, exchange, and so on—and in it he talks about a natural self-love.

The potential conflict between the two books is evident: What motivates human beings—sympathy or self-love? Some early scholars thought that Smith had a change of heart between the publication of his first book (when he was 36), which speaks of sympathy, and the publication of his second (when he was 53), which speaks of self-love. As an idealistic young man he may have thought, "Oh, well, we all have sympathy for one another." And then, after he had been around the block, he went to France and discovered that the motivator is not altruism and sympathy at all, it is self-love.

Are there multiple conceptions of human motivation? If so, are they competing? How do these two things go together? Can you be both a moral person and an economic agent?

I always tell my students that before you can criticize a book, you need to understand it. The principle of charity is to understand, and put in the best light possible, an author's arguments. Smith was a very smart man and he revised his two books several times during his lifetime. In fact he would revise them both—at the same time, right next to each other—throughout many years of his life. If a major contradiction existed between the two books, one would assume that he would have seen it. But he didn't. He did not think that the books were contradictory.

Allow me to point you to several passages. This is from *The Theory of Moral Sentiments*: "And hence it is, that to feel much for others and little for ourselves, that to restrain our selfish, and to indulge our benevolent affections, constitutes the perfection of human nature" (TMS I.i.5.5). Note what he said in the *Wealth of Nations*. "Self-love the governing principle in the intercourse* of human society" (Smith's index to WN 3/e). I put an asterisk by the word "intercourse" because I will return to it later.

One could be forgiven for thinking that two different conceptions of human behavior are being discussed in those two passages, or perhaps two different conceptions of human virtue. The question of how economics and ethics can go together is one we are confronted with today, and this is not merely as an abstract conversation in an ivory tower. This is something that a humane society, which I hope we all want, needs to understand. Smith's problem is also our problem.

So, do Smith's two books work in concert? Yes, they do.

I think each book applies the same explanatory model to different large-scale human social institutions. What Smith was trying to do was understand the phenomenon of human moral judgment-making, and this led him to observe and understand, as a scientist might, that human beings are creating social institutions all the time. A scientist viewing these kinds of phenomena might be able to see patterns that might explain how they came into being and how they change over time, that might explain how they are maintained and how they decay.

I propose that Smith develops an explanatory model of human morality and applies it in *The Theory of Moral Sentiments*. In the *Wealth of Nations* he then applies a similar model to another human social institution, namely what we think of now as economic behavior.

Smith noticed that the same model applies to both—and potentially applies to other large-scale human social institutions, including language, law, perhaps even science.

What Smith did in *The Theory of Moral Sentiments* was create a social science. Though usually considered the father of economics, I think perhaps a better way to think of Adam Smith is as the father of social science.

Can there actually be a science of human behavior? This is something of a live question. When determining whether, in fact, there can be a science applied to human behavior the way a science can be applied to non-human or non-sentient behavior, one must consider the concept of free will, a concept that makes it more difficult to predict what a human being might do. You can predict with scientific accuracy what an inert object might do, but—factoring in free will—can the same be true of a human being?

Smith thought that, yes, we could have a proper social science based on what the fixed features of human nature. Indeed, he thought this would be a Newtonian project. In the eighteenth century, Newton was a scientist, philosopher, and natural philosopher par excellence: He had unlocked secrets. Smith thought Newtonian methodology—observing phenomena to discover patterns that could describe the regular behavior of the phenomena—could be applied to the human social world.

Let us look more specifically at the moral theory in *The Moral Theory of Sentiments*. Smith thought that we all had an innate natural desire for what he calls the "mutual sympathy of sentiments." By "sympathy" he did not mean pity, feeling sorry for someone. What he meant was that we have a sympathy of sentiments if our sentiments are roughly the same, if they are in "concord," or "harmony," other words Smith used.

Another more controversial aspect of Smith's argument is that he believed we develop and train our moral sentiments over time. He did not believe we are born with our full panoply of moral sentiments. We are born with some natural instincts, including particularly the desire for mutual sympathy of sentiments, but our moral sentiments evolve over time via interactions with others. What this meant to Smith is that communities will tend to have overlapping systems of moral sentiments, but also that people from very different experiences might have some differences in their moral sentiments.

I want to emphasize that for Smith moral judgment is a skill. Here I think he is in the Aristotelian camp. You become virtuous by practicing virtue. Moral judgment is improved by making moral judgments. As a somewhat separate issue, I think this has potential political and policy implications, that the degree to which we prevent people from feeling the consequences of their decisions will enfeeble their moral judgment-making skill.

Smith noticed that human beings spend a lot of time judging one another. We don't always communicate our judgments, but we do make them constantly: judgments based on how people are dressed, how they talk—and what they talk about, the music they listen to ... the list is endless. To a certain profound extent, then, to be human is to judge others. Now that doesn't mean it is bad, even if the judgments aren't always fair. It just means that judging others is part of being human.

But here is another consideration. We are able to follow many more rules of moral judgment than we realize. Take laughing, one of Smith's favorite examples. Are there rules about laughing? Are there rules about joke telling? Are there rules about what kinds of jokes are appropriate under certain circumstances? Absolutely! But can you lay out all the rules about what types of jokes are appropriate when, and which are not? That is not easy to do. But, it doesn't mean the rules don't exist. In fact, not only do they exist, they are ruthlessly enforced. Suppose you are with a group of friends and someone tells a joke that is mildly funny: You all give a little laugh—except for one person who laughs a bit too long. Well, how long is too long? And supposed this happens again a while later. Is something going on here? Is this person not quite with it, or has he had a few too many drinks, or he is trying to get a date, maybe a job? There has to be some extenuating circumstance to explain his actions.

As you observe these rules, occasionally you will find people who will "push the envelope" or "cross the line a bit." You could think of these people as entrepreneurs in a way. They are trying something new to see if there is any sympathy of sentiments for it out there or not.

What was interesting to Smith is not the precise content of the rules, but rather the fact that the rules exist. But who exactly is developing and codifying and enforcing the rules? As yet there are no federal bureaus of laughter, so who is the central authority? We are. Human beings do it all on their own. That is what Smith noticed, and that is the key to the mechanism that he is about to unlock.

Let's look at children. Adam Smith never married, he never had children. He says some things about children that only a childless person would ever say. For example, he said that until the ages of seven or eight, children are basically indistinguishable, they are all the same. That is obviously incorrect, but some of his other statements about children are right on the money. Smith noticed that babies have no sense of right or wrong, they just have wants and needs. They have no sense of what is proper to ask for and what is not. Smith suggests that for the first few years of their lives, caregivers often indulge their charges by satisfying what might be thought of as outrageous demands. But then, he says, there comes the time when a child ventures out and begins to spend time with other children. It is then that the child has the rude and unsettling experience of realizing that he or she is no longer the center of everyone's life. Only his own. Other children don't feel the need— nor do they have the obligation—to indulge the child the way parents and family might. Smith suggests that rebukes from one's playmates awaken the desire for mutual sympathy of sentiments. He calls this the "great school of self-command." If you demand that other children satisfy your demands, it is likely they will rebuke you and leave—not a pleasant experience. So, almost unwittingly, the child begins to search out ways to alter his or her behavior so that a sympathy of sentiments can be achieved. When that happens, when you have that experience fairly early in life, this begins, according to Smith, a lifelong search for conventions, habits, rules, eventually principles of behavior that will enhance the chances of achieving mutual sympathy of sentiments. Over time the individual develops a sophisticated set of principles that guide behavior. These range from what we think of as moral principles proper to rules of etiquette. Eventually normal human beings will develop what is called a conscience. And the conscience is, for Smith, the background sense of the principles that determines proper codes of behavior.

At that last stage, what we get is the development of a standard of morality that Smith calls the "impartial spectator" (he also termed this "the man within the breast" and "God's vice gérant upon earth"). You always have the impartial spectator on your shoulder assessing your behavior. When you are contemplating whether or not to do X, this impartial spectator—the observer who has no particular stake in what you do and who will not benefit either way—speaks to you. This becomes for Smith a kind of heuristic device. This is where Smith does make a recommendation, where he was writing to the young, enterprising, intelligent Scotsman of the eighteenth century. If you want to be a morally upright person and if you want to have a chance of leading a good and happy life—which will include deep and affectionate relations with other people—ask yourself, what would such an observer think of my behavior?

Now, whose voice is that really? If you know something about Aristotle's moral theory, it may be akin to what he called the *phronemos*, the virtuous man. It might also be the voice of God.

So Smith believe that morality develops over the lifespan of each human being. Gradually each one of us gets better at anticipating how others will react to our behavior. We incorporate these responses into our own set of rules about how to act. Our many attempts to reach mutual sympathy of sentiments lead first to habits of behavior, then to principles that guide our conscience.

This might suggest twenty-first-century social science. Micro intentions lead to macro results. What I mean by that is that all any particular individual has in mind at any particular moment is achieving a mutual sympathy of sentiments with his or her immediate group. Typically we are not thinking about larger patterns of behavior. Nevertheless our collective attempts to achieve mutual sympathy of sentiments give rise to larger patterns of behavior that the moral philosopher, or what we now might think of as a social scientist, can observe. Micro, or local, intentions give rise to macro, or global, results.

The development depends, necessarily, on interactions with others. If you never have interactions with other humans, then, according to Smith, you will never develop truly moral sentiments. In *The Theory of Moral Sentiments*, he includes a thought experiment. Imagine a person who grew up on an island all by himself (this is counterfactual for Smith), with no interaction with other human beings whatsoever. Would such a person be able to develop moral sentiments? Smith's answer is no. That person might have a sense of pain after he stubs his toe, or taste when he finds a patch of berries, but he would have not properly developed moral sentiments because that requires human interaction.

The effect of having these properly developed moral sentiments is the creation of a social system that is a kind of spontaneous order. That is a modern phrase, not one that Smith would have used, but I think it accurately describes what Smith has in mind when he writes about large-scale human social institutions including morality. I think this means a marketplace of morality.

What we see in the development of systems of moral behavior are six specific features that are also features of markets more generally. What we see is a single principle—it is not the only one, but it is the principal motivating desire—the mutual sympathy of sentiments. In the marketplace, things are exchanged. Some of the things exchanged are sentiments, our judgments of one another. There is also competition because we cannot simultaneously sympathize with everybody. When people have competing sentiments, we have to select with whom we are going to sympathize and with whom we are not. This introduces a competitive element, because since we all want this, and it becomes a kind of scarce resource, we compete for it. What happens is the spontaneous development of rules, Smith calls them the rules of propriety, the rules of merit. We then have a spontaneous order. Shared standards of morality.

You might say this sounds like a naturalistic account of human morality, which to some extent it is, but does it allow for objectivity? The kind of objectivity that I believe Smith thinks this system can generate is what we might call intersubjective objectivity. That is, the moral rules are not up to any one of us. No one of us can just willy-nilly change the moral rules. They are up to all of us. You might think of the value of currency in the same way. That we use little green pieces of paper as opposed to other things to represent our currency—that was our collective choice.

Compare the six principles of Marketplace of Morality with the six principles of the Marketplace of Economics.

Marketplace of Morality Principles

1. *Motivating desire*: "pleasure of mutual sympathy"
2. *Market*: sentiments, judgments
3. *Competition*: striving for limited sympathy

4. *Rules developed*: "propriety," "merit"
5. *Spontaneous order*: shared standards of morality
6. *Objectivity*: overlapping consensus, impartial spectator's judgment

Marketplace of Economics Principles

1. *Motivating desire*: "natural effort of every individual to better his own condition"
2. *Market*: goods, services
3. *Competition*: striving for scarce resources
4. *Rules developed*: "justice"—"life and person," "property and possessions," and "personal rights"
5. *Spontaneous order*: economy—intricate, dynamic network of exchanges of goods, services
6. *Objectivity*: property, contract, prices

Notice that they are same six features, although instantiated by slightly different elements. Both have a principal motivating desire: in the market case, "the natural effort of every individual to better his own condition." (That is a quote from the *Wealth of Nations*.) In this case, goods and services are being traded. What is the competition? Once again, striving for scarce resources. And again, rules develop, which Smith refers to as rules of justice. Smith thinks that there are just three rules of justice: (1) respecting the life and person of another, (2) respecting the property and possessions of another, and (3) respecting personal rights or voluntary contracts.

Hadn't others—John Locke, for example—already written these rules out very carefully, deducing them from natural law? Maybe, but what Smith thinks is that given human nature, given the circumstances that human beings find themselves in, unless there is some artificial interference in the development of their social orders, they will develop these rules because human interaction and the chances for human prosperity are increased if we follow these rules. There is, again, a system of spontaneous order and then there is also an objectivity—property, contract, and prices. Smith believes that prices have a kind of inter-subjective objectivity. For example, it is certainly true that high-definition televisions cost one amount five years ago and that they cost a different amount today, but what they cost today is not up to you or me or any other single person. Prices are set by negotiations, or as Smith says, "the higgling and bargaining of the market," and incorporate all sorts of features that no one of us can fully comprehend or be responsible for.

What I suggest in solving the Adam Smith problem is that we have the same model for human social institutions in both of Smith's books. We have the same marketplace model. This allows us to have a creditable social science based on the common core features of human nature and on the overlapping features of human circumstances. What this also implies is a kind of presumptive respect for the rules that have developed in this way. It is not absolute, because after all, new experiences, entrepreneurship—both moral and economic—might give rise to slightly new patterns of behavior, slightly new ways of allocating resources: moral sentiments/sympathy on the one hand, natural resources on the other. Nevertheless, these rules deserve a kind of presumptive authority because they incorporate the numberless experiences and experiments of previous generations.

Smith's model applies to language as well. In the eighteenth century there was considerable speculation on the origins of language, and Smith wrote an essay about it. How is it that human beings have language and other animals don't? Rousseau, for example, thought that there was no way that we could explain it naturally because in order to have language, human beings had to have the capacity for abstract thought, but in order to have the capacity for abstract thought, we had to have language. Unable to get out of this problem, Rousseau decided it had to be a miracle. But for Smith, language itself is just another spontaneous order. What may appear to be a perfectly designed set of institutions is likely something that could have arisen in exactly the same marketplace via the same marketplace mechanism. There is a level of objectivity. New usages arise, languages change over time. That is part and parcel of its living nature.

What I would like to suggest is that *The Theory of Moral Sentiments* is important because from it we get a grand unification theory for all human social institutions, for human sociality generally. That is a pretty impressive feat. Smith attempted to work out a similar model for other large-scale human social institutions, including the history of law, common law included. Because he hadn't quite worked the model out to his satisfaction before he died, he burned 16 volumes of manuscript to avoid their publication.

But his grand unification theory provides a single model that explains the development and maintenance and change over time of human social institutions. I call understanding these institutions a marketplace of life. All are based on the interactions that I have described and all share the same six features. Smith was among the first to effectively inaugurate a profound new school of thinking about human social institutions, sometimes called the Scottish Historical School, an empirically and observationally based attempt to understand human sociality. It turns out that many researchers today are rediscovering elements of the very model that Smith observed. There are a number of people who see the Smithian spontaneous order model, which I call the marketplace model, in the development of language. It turns out there is a considerable and growing amount of evidence that we really do desire mutual sympathy of sentiments and it may, after all, be the single greatest social desire we have.

Earlier in this essay, I set up *Das Adam Smith Problem*, examining the motivations behind his two books. To what degree does self-interest motivate us and to what degree do other factors motivate us? One other aspect of the argument that *The Theory of Moral Sentiments* presents is very important to Adam Smith and for understanding his concept. I call it the familiarity principle, and what this means is that our natural concern for other people is determined in large part by our familiarity with them. The more time we spend with someone, the more we are inclined to take an interest in what affects that person. We become more and more concerned with people as we become more and more familiar with them, and of course, the converse is true as well. If our concern for others varies with familiarity, we are most concerned, Smith determined, with ourselves and our closest family members. We grow less concerned with distance: extended family members, friends, acquaintances, strangers. This has many implications for Smith. One is something we may think of as moral cosmopolitanism, a moral view that some philosophers hold today that we should have just as much concern for any human being as we have for any particular human being. One of my former colleagues is the son of the philosopher James Rachels, who argued that there is no morally justifiable reason for preferring the success of your own children to the success of any other child. That there is no moral reason why you should be more concerned about your own children than anyone else's.

Whatever you think about the moral value, the moral status of that claim, for Smith it is naturally impossible for the reason that our love, our concern, is a scarce resource. We don't have an unlimited amount of love and concern. Indeed, it might be one of our most important resources, and it has to be treated as such—it has to be very carefully allocated. The way to most effectively do that is to distribute it to the people that you are most familiar with, the people with whom you can most effectively help.

In economics most of our trading is with strangers. Chances are you have no idea who made your clothes or your electronic devices. For you to have as much concern for them as you do for your own family— even to claim such a thing—is, for Smith, not naturally possible. And, according to Smith, it is not even recommended because all it will do is dissipate your love in ways that cannot be requited.

In the marketplace of economics, the behavior that is required of us is self-interest within the bounds of justice. Smith thinks you have to observe the three rules of justice with everyone—whether you know them or not. Actions beyond that, however, are dependent only on your degree of familiarity with those involved. "Self-love," as Smith said, "is the governing principle in the intercourse of human society." In the nineteenth century, "intercourse" meant human interactions that have to do soley and specifically with commerce. In his *Theory of Moral Sentiments*, Smith famously wrote: "We may often fulfill all the rules of justice by sitting still and doing nothing." That is a simple yet profound statement. By sitting quietly in a theater watching a movie, you are respecting absolutely every other person in the room. You are acting with justice toward each of them by not assaulting them, stealing from them, or violating their agreements. And you can do that just by sitting still. Do you owe people anything more than that? Possibly, but that will depend on the degree to which you are familiar with them and their situation, necessary information if you are to offer significant assistance.

In conclusion, let me make three points: (1) *The Theory of Moral Sentiments'* marketplace model unifies Smith's work. It provides a single model for all human social institutions. (2) There is a great deal, and ever-increasing amount, of contemporary research from multiple disciplines that supports this model. (3) Smith's model offers a deep connection between economics and morality that is based on human sociality. This is a rather remarkable feat for someone working in eighteenth-century Scotland, writing by himself.

So do markets and morality mix? Not only do they mix, but to have a comprehensive humane social science, they must.

ROY C. SMITH

Adam Smith and the Creation
of the American Economy

Some years ago, while researching a book on wealth creation, it became obvious to me that the United States stood out from all other countries in the world for its continuous and enduring ability to generate national wealth, or what Adam Smith called "opulence." I began to wonder why that was. What was it about the United States that made it stand out as it did?

The British had colonized other large landmasses—Canada and Australia, for example. France and Russia had undergone "revolutions," and Latin America had broken away from Spanish rule in the nineteenth century. But none of them had developed a vibrant entrepreneurial economic system that was capable of attracting a steady flow of both immigrants and investment capital looking for a better way.

Our system did, but why? Why us?

When I asked around, some said that this was the product of the "Protestant Work Ethic"—except that there were many more Protestants in Europe than in America in the 1800s. Some suggested the cause was the special "get up and go" of immigrants—except that during the 169 years of immigration under colonial rule our economy did not develop as it did afterward. Others claimed it was the American "entrepreneurial spirit" that made the difference. This makes sense only if you recognize the unique national economic system that the spirit was enabled to work within. That system was the genius of the American experience, and the genius behind it was Adam Smith.

Though he never visited this country, Adam Smith had enormous belief in it. Ever the economist, Smith believed the discovery of America was one of the two most important achievements of man in the history of the world (the other was the discovery of the eastern trade route around Cape Horn). But what Adam Smith had to say about America, and the rest of his outline for the budding science of economics, was aimed at the British, not the Americans.

What he had to say in 1776, when *Wealth of Nations* was published, was that the British economic system of the eighteenth century, though the most effective in the world, suffered from serious defects and misunderstandings that not only prevented it from improving its own opulence, but also from developing the opulence of America.

His great work, now regarded as a classic of the Enlightenment, was praised in England by a few scholars, but dismissed as impractical by most politicians and statesmen. After the French Revolution in 1789, it was criticized as being full of seditious ideas that were dangerous to British social stability. His ideas were not taken seriously by anyone involved in British economic policies for at least another fifty years.

But these ideas were devoured in America by those seeking new approaches to politics, governance, and economics. All of the Founding Fathers were familiar with *Wealth of Nations*; some had copies sent to them hot off the press. In America several of his most profound ideas, radical for his time, were put to work almost immediately. The Revolutionary War ended in 1783, and the new United States was governed by the Articles of Confederation until the Constitution was adopted in 1789. During that period, the states operated under a weak and ineffective federal arrangement that was not much better than the wartime Continental Congress, but it did provide an important learning experience for the new republic. Without a much stronger federal system, most of the framers had to agree, the not-very-United States were likely to go bankrupt, shake themselves apart arguing over disputes, and/or become so weak as to invite reoccupation by Britain or some other European power. The new Constitution was a remedy to the defects of Confederation, but there were many devils lurking in the details.

The implementation of the economic powers of the Constitution was left to the boy wonder of the Revolution, 33-year-old Alexander Hamilton, who had long since mastered Adam Smith's work and borrowed four key ideas from it that have become—despite some erosion here and there—the load-bearing pillars of the American economic system ever since.

Four Great Ideas

Free Markets

The first great idea was the commitment to free markets to serve as the principal allocator of investment assets.

In Britain and the rest of Europe, land was the principal source of wealth in the eighteenth century. It provided most of the jobs and produced most of the food that society consumed. But, according to Adam Smith, the "market" for land and labor was far from free: It was constricted by layer upon layer of ancient privileges, feudal rights, and local customs that obstructed access to land and the mobility of labor, while concentrating political power in the hands of landowners. To be free, and thus "fair," all markets had to be governed by natural laws of supply and demand, and contain the freedom for individuals to pursue their self-interest.

Neither the Constitution nor the sentiment of the people provided room for privileges, and whatever colonial customs existed were abolished, so free markets emerged more or less naturally. But they didn't have to, and there were many temptations to do things differently.

The Treaty of Paris that ended the war with Britain doubled the land area of the United States, extending it from the Alleghenies to the Mississippi. It included unsettled land that the British had not wanted to defend against Indian resistance to Western expansion. Some of this land, which in aggregate represented the new country's greatest source of wealth by far, might have been awarded as grants to those best able to finance its development—that is, to the richest, such as Robert Morris, John Jacob Astor, Steven Girard, or Moses Brown. Or, some—there was a lot to go around—might have awarded to the great generals or political leaders of the Revolution, as had long been the practice in Europe, making George Washington an even greater landowner in Ohio than he already was, or ceding parts of Maine to Samuel Adams or John Hancock. The land, too, might have been used as a means for settling debts or obligations of the government, even perhaps to some foreign creditors. All were fairly common practices in Europe.

Americans completely rejected such practices as being too close to the monarchial system they had just overthrown. The land was, instead, auctioned over time to those who would settle and develop it, including some rich families, but everyone had to pay market prices, and many went bankrupt in the process. Nevertheless the vast amount of land controlled by the government was distributed, probably for the first time in modern history, in accordance with free market forces.

Free Trade

The second great idea was Adam Smith's notion of free trade, which would develop the practice of comparative advantage that treated both sides to a win–win outcome.

Britain was a trading nation, Smith said, but its trade was largely one-sided, tied to the mercantile system that it employed with its colonies. This was the system that required British manufacturers, British prices, British bottoms (i.e., ships), and British finance. It was designed to collect most of the profits from trading in Britain; the colonies were allowed to grow by expanding their exports, but not much faster.

The Americans never quite cottoned on to how uneven the mercantile system was: They appreciated British markets for their commodities, and were eager to import British manufactured goods. Their rebellious objections were to taxes unilaterally imposed on them by Parliament— they accepted taxes voted by their own elected legislatures—but the British insisted on the right to tax them from London to defray the cost of their military and other commitments. In British terms, these costs were small in relation to the gains they received from the mercantile system.

Adam Smith saw the inconsistency in the British position, calling America a nation of "customers" that British mistreatment foolishly had driven away. His vision of America included its becoming the voting part of the United Kingdom, and ending the mercantile practices that had stunted its growth. After a century or so of allocating seats in

Parliament on the basis of wealth or population, Britain, he believed, would see that the economic center of gravity of the United Kingdom had shifted westward. In time, he said, Britain's capital city would have to shift also, perhaps to some place like Pittsburgh, which was named for William Pitt the Elder in appreciation for his pro-American position in opposition to King George.

The fledgling United States, a trading nation with no colonies, was naturally for free trade, but had to struggle to get it from Britain and other counterparties after the war. Its primary source of federal revenue was custom collections, so tariffs and other duties were important. On the whole the country has adhered to the principles of free trade and open markets, despite backsliding from time to time over the years.

Solid Money

The third great idea emphasized the importance of money and credit in the economy.

Alexander Hamilton devised the U.S. currency and the operating system for American banking and lending, and he persuaded a reluctant Congress to create a central bank to monitor and control it. Hamilton's *Report on the Public Credit*, a masterpiece that imported ideas and arguments from Adam Smith, the Bank of England (chartered in 1694), and other prominent European financial figures and institutions, was the blueprint for the system that assumed the debts of the states, provided loans to banks, established markets in government securities, and repaired the damage to American credit imposed on it by the Articles of Confederation. The credit system, however, faced strong resistance from Thomas Jefferson and others fearful that the Federalists would abuse the powers provided to the new government at the expense of the southern and more agrarian parts of the country. Hamilton won out, but Congress did not renew the charter of his Bank of the United States, which President James Madison opposed, when it expired in 1811.

However, a Second Bank of the United States was chartered in 1816, after America's finances, struggling to pay for the War of 1812, fell into disrepair. But the Second Bank's charter was not renewed in 1836 when it expired, this time with President Andrew Jackson opposing it, considering it discriminated against rural parts of the country. The

Federal Reserve System was not established until 1913, so America's history of orderly money and banking has been quite uneven. But, in the beginning, the Hamiltonian system worked effectively and got the country started. After that, free markets somewhat haphazardly controlled the availability of credit.

Manufacturing

The last great idea of Adam Smith to be adopted in the United States was the importance of manufacturers to its developing economy. Smith's ideas about the economies of scale from the specialization of labor, and his vision of a factory system, appeared extensively in Hamilton's second masterpiece, *Report on Manufacturers*. Though this report recommended that the government provide initial "bonuses" or grants to manufacturing start-ups (which Congress did not adopt), the vision became the reality as market forces provided the demand for manufactured goods previously imported, technology advanced, and labor and capital were allocated to factories and distribution.

Adam Smith died in 1790, the same year as Benjamin Franklin (whom he had met in France), just as the United States was starting on an economic progression that Smith expected to be tremendous. The Industrial Revolution began around the same time, and it would accelerate America's growth manyfold. It increased the prosperity of the industrialized north to the point of overtaking the economic power of the slave-driven southern states, which ultimately enabled the Civil War to be won and slavery to be ended.

If Adam Smith were to visit the United States today, he would be pleased to discover that his four guiding principles—Free Markets, Free Trade, Solid Money, and Manufacturing—have helped to produce the opulence we have today. He would understand that the principles are challenged by politics from time to time, and suffer abuses occasionally, but they always recover as things change and the principles are rediscovered.

He probably would be surprised by the extent to which the voting franchise in America has been so greatly expanded and would probably expect that a growing democracy would require its government to provide more services than perhaps, optimally, it should. But, at the same time, he would be able to contrast that observation with the memory of his own time in which very small voting franchises protected uneconomic privileges and other practices far longer than they should have.

If asked what he thought of Europe's economic situation today, he might reply that the European Union has come a long way in improving its markets and trade practices and in allowing manufacturing to overtake agriculture. Its current experiment in money and credit, however, resembles too much the American confederation period and only a federalizing of debt, budgets, and fiscal activity, as was done in eighteenth-century Britain and America, will enable that union to sustain itself.

MARK SKOUSEN

The Centrality of the Invisible Hand

> Adam Smith had one overwhelmingly important triumph:
> he put into the *center* of economics the systematic analysis of
> the behavior of individuals pursuing their self-interest under
> conditions of competition.
>
> —George Stigler[1]

A major debate has flared up recently about Adam Smith. Was he the
father of free-market economics and libertarian thought, or was he
some kind of radical egalitarian and social democrat?

Adam Smith as a Free-Market Hero

The traditional view, held by Milton Friedman, is that the Scottish
philosopher was "a radical and a revolutionary in his time—just as
those of us who preach laissez faire are in our time."[2] He lauded Smith's
metaphor of the "invisible hand," the famous Smithian idea that "by
pursuing his own self interest, [every individual] frequently promotes
that of the society."[3] According to Friedman, "Adam Smith's flash of
genius was his recognition that the prices that emerged from voluntary
transactions between buyers and seller—for short, in a free market—

49

could coordinate the activity of millions of people, each seeking his own interest, in such a way as to make everyone better off."[4] Other defenders of free-enterprise capitalism describe the invisible hand as "gentle," "wise," "far reaching," and one that "improves the lives of others."[5]

George Stigler, Friedman's colleague at the University of Chicago, identified the invisible hand doctrine as "the crown jewel" and first principle of welfare economics, "the most important substantive proposition in all of economics."[6] He waxed eloquently about the "grandparent" of modern economics, his "bold explorations, his resourceful detective work..., his duels and triumphs and defeats.... [his] superior mind... a clear-eyed and tough-minded observer.... *The Wealth of Nations* has joined the great literature of all time; it was the most powerful assault ever launched against the mercantile philosophy that dominated Western Europe from 1500 to 1800."[7] Adam Smith was Stigler's favorite economist, and a portrait of the Chicago economist holding a copy of the *Wealth of Nations* hangs in the hallway of the business school at Chicago.

This is one area where the Austrians Ludwig von Mises and Friedrich Hayek concurred with the Chicago School. Like Stigler, Mises wrote an introduction to the *Wealth of Nations*, calling it a "great book." According to Mises, Smith's works are "the consummation, summarization, and perfection...of a marvelous system of ideas...presented with admirable logical clarity and an impeccable literary form.... [representing] the essence of the ideology of freedom, individualism, and prosperity." Furthermore, "Its publication date—1776—marks the dawn of freedom both political and economic.... It paved the way for the unprecedented achievements of laissez-faire capitalism." He concluded, "There can hardly be found another book that could initiate a man better into the study of the history of modern ideas and the prosperity created by industrialization."[8]

In like manner, Hayek wrote a laudatory article on the 200th anniversary of the publication date of the *Wealth of Nations*. After praising earlier economists and warning of defects in Smith's value and distribution theories, he went on to extol Smith as "the greatest of them all" because the Scottish economist, more than any of his contemporaries or ancestors, recognized that "a man's efforts will benefit more people, and on the whole satisfy greater needs, when he lets himself be guided by the abstract signals of prices rather than perceived needs," and thus Smith helped to create a "great society."[9]

Social Democrats Contest the Free Marketeers

Critics of laissez faire—from Cambridge economist Emma Rothschild to British Labor Party leader Gordon Brown—have recently become quite unhappy by what they consider a conspiracy by free marketeers to claim Adam Smith as their hero and symbol of laissez faire. They seem to be especially annoyed that the Adam Smith Institute, a London-based free-market think tank, erected a popular statue of the grand old man on Mile High Street in Edinburgh on July 4, 2008.

In a series of books and articles, they have attempted to wrestle Adam Smith out of the hands of the free-market arena and into the camp of the social democrats. According to Oxford professor Iain McLean and Illinois professor Samuel Fleschaker, the Scottish philosopher was a "radical egalitarian" who, while endorsing economic liberalism, had a lively appreciation of market failure and ultimately rejected "ruthless laissez-faire capitalism" in favor of "human equality" and "distributive justice."[10]

These revisionists are quick to claim that Smith was no friend of rent-seeking landlords, monopolistic merchants, and conspiring businessmen, and that he advocated an active state authority in support of free education, large-scale public works, usury laws, progressive taxation, and even some limits on free trade. They contend that Smith had more in common with Karl Marx than Thomas Jefferson.[11]

The critics of laissez faire offer a mixed review of Smith's invisible hand. In their Keynesian textbook, William Baumol and Alan Blinder admit that "the invisible hand has an astonishing capacity to handle a coordination problem of truly enormous proportions."[12] Despite expecting anarchic chaos, Frank Hahn discovers spontaneous order in Adam Smith's marketplace. He honors the invisible hand theory as "astonishing," noting "whatever criticisms I shall level at the theory later, I should like to record that it is a major intellectual achievement.... The invisible hand works in harmony [that] leads to the growth in the output of goods which people desire."[13]

And yet despite these words of praise, Smith's wonderful world is full of inefficiencies, waste, and imperfections. Accordingly, the public must beware of the "backhand," "the trembling hand," the "bloody hand," the "iron fist of competition," a hand "getting stuck," and perhaps even a hand that may need to be "amputated."[14]

To emphasize the imperfections of the marketplace, mainstream publishers have mostly assign big-government advocates to write the introductions to the popular editions of the *Wealth of Nations*, including Marx Lerner and Robert Reich for the Modern Library editions, and Alan B. Krueger for the Bantam paperback edition, where he labels Adam Smith as a follower not of Milton Friedman but of John Rawls; his invisible hand is seen as "all thumbs."[15]

Murray Rothbard's Dissent

The political waters have been muddied a bit since libertarian Murray Rothbard and his followers have joined the critics in their attack on Adam Smith (one of a few examples where Rothbard parts company with Mises and Hayek). Rothbard took exception to the celebrated Adam Smith in his two-volume history of economic thought, published at the time of Rothbard's death in 1995. He lambasted the classical economists, arguing that Smith apostatized from the sound doctrines and theories previously developed by pre-Adamites such as Richard Cantillion, Anne Robert Turgot, and the Spanish scholastics. He asserted that Adam Smith's contributions were "dubious" at best, that "he originated nothing that was true, and that whatever he originated was wrong," and that the *Wealth of Nations* was "rife with vagueness, ambiguity and deep inner contradictions." Specifically, his doctrine of value was an "unmitigated disaster"; his theory of distribution was "disastrous"; his emphasis on the long run was a "tragic detour"; and Smith's putative "sins" include support for progressive taxation, fractional reserve banking, and a crude labor theory of value that Marxists later borrowed from Adam Smith and David Ricardo.[16]

Adam Smith Reveals the Invisible Hand

What about the metaphor of the "invisible hand," the famous Smithian idea that "by pursuing his own self interest, [every individual] frequently promotes that of the society"?[17] Free-market economists from Ludwig von Mises to Milton Friedman have regarded it as a powerful symbol of unfettered market forces, what Adam Smith called his "system of natural liberty." In rebuttal, the new critics belittle Adam Smith's metaphor as a "passing, satirical" reference and suggest that he favored more of a "helping hand."[18] They emphasize the fact that Smith used the phrase "invisible hand" only once in each of his two major works, *The Theory of Moral Sentiments* (1759) and the *Wealth of Nations* (1776). The references are so sparse that commentators seldom mentioned the expression by name in the nineteenth century. No notice was made of it during the celebrations of the centenary of the *Wealth of Nations* in 1876. In the eighteenth and nineteenth centuries, no subject index, including the well-known volume edited by Edwin Cannan, published in 1904, lists "invisible hand" as a separate entry. It was finally added to the subject index in 1937 by Max Lerner for the Modern Library edition. Clearly, it wasn't until the twentieth century that the invisible hand became a popular symbol of laissez faire.

Invisible Hand: Marginal or Central Concept?

Could the detractors be correct in their assessment of Adam Smith's sentiments? Is the invisible hand metaphor central or marginal to Adam Smith's "system of natural liberty"?

Milton Friedman refers to Adam Smith's symbol as a "key insight" into the cooperative, self-regulating "power of the market to produce our food, our clothing, our housing…without central direction."[19] George Stigler calls it the "crown jewel" of the *Wealth of Nations* and "the most important substantive proposition in all of economics."[20] The idea that laissez faire leads to the common good is called "the first fundamental theorem of welfare economics" by Kenneth Arrow, Paul Samuelson, and Ronald Coase.[21]

On the other hand, Gavin Kennedy contended in earlier writings that the invisible hand is nothing more than an afterthought, a "casual metaphor" with limited value.[22] Emma Rothschild even goes so far as to declare, "What I will suggest is that Smith did not especially esteem the invisible hand…. It is un-Smithian and unimportant to his theory" and was nothing more than a "mildly ironic joke."[23]

Who's right?

Adam Smith Reveals His Invisible Hand

A fascinating discovery uncovered by Daniel Klein, professor of economics at George Mason University, may shed light on this debate. Based on a brief remark by Peter Minowitz that the "invisible hand" phrase lies roughly in the middle of both the *Wealth of Nations* and *The Theory of Moral Sentiments*,[24] Klein made preliminary investigations that led him to suggest deliberate centrality.[25] Klein recruited Brandon Lucas, then a doctoral student at George Mason, to investigate further. Klein and Lucas found considerable evidence that Smith "deliberately placed 'led by an invisible hand' at the centre of his tomes" and that the concept "holds special and positive significance in Smith's thought."[26]

Klein and Lucas base their conjecture on two major points. First, the physical location of the metaphor: The single expression "led by an invisible hand" occurs almost dead center in the first and second editions of the *Wealth of Nations*. (It moves slightly away from the middle after an index and additions were added to later editions.)

Moreover, it appears again "well-nigh dead centre" in the final edition of *The Theory of Moral Sentiments*. Klein and Lucas admit that it was not in the middle of the first edition in 1759, speculating that "physical centrality was not initially a part of his intentions...[but that] by 1776, Smith had become intent on centrality." Indeed, Smith moved the phrase "invisible hand" closer to the center of the book, first by appending an important essay on the origin of language and finally by making substantial revisions in the final edition.[27]

Second, Klein and Lucas note that as an historian and moral philosopher, Adam Smith commented frequently on the importance of middleness in architecture, literature, science, and philosophy. For example:

- Smith wrote sympathetically about the Aristotelian golden mean, the idea that virtue exists "between two opposite vices." For instance, between the two extremes of cowardice and recklessness lies the central virtue of courage.

- In Smith's essays on astronomy and ancient physics, Smith was captivated by Newtonian central forces and periodic revolutions.

- Klein discovered that Smith, in his lectures on rhetoric, admired the poetry of the Greek poet Thycydides, who "often expresses all that he labours so much in a word or two, sometimes placed in the middle of the narration."[28]

Midpoint analysis and centralized themes existed long before Adam Smith's time. For example, the Talmud offers considerable commentary about midpoints in the Torah, especially in a poetic form called *chiasmus*. *Chiasmus* is characterized by introverted parallelism, and found in Greek, Latin, Hebrew, and Christian literature. A *chiasmus* is a pattern of words or ideas stated once and then stated again *but in reverse order*. Classic examples are found in the Bible: "Who *sheds* the *blood* of a *man*, by a *man* shall his *blood* be *shed*..." (Genesis 9:6), or "The *first* shall be *last* and the *last* shall be *first*..." (Matthew 19:30) [emphasis added].

Most *chiasmi* have a "climactic centrality," that is, the structure of the poem points to a central theme in the middle. For instance, the Psalmist writes, "Our soul is *escaped* as a bird out of the *snare* of the *fowlers*; the *snare* is broken, and we are *escaped*." (Psalms 124:7) [emphasis added] Here the Psalmist is urging us (the soul) to escape the clutches of Satan, even as a bird escapes the snare of the fowler or the hunter (the central word).

The standard pattern of a centralized *chiamus* is:

$$A$$
$$B$$
$$C \text{ (central theme or focal point)}$$
$$B$$
$$A$$

In sum, according to Klein and Lucas, the invisible hand represents the climatic centrality of Smith's "system of natural liberty," and is appropriately found in the middle of his works. By this discovery, if true, one goes from one extreme to the other—from seeing the invisible hand as a marginal concept to accepting it as the touchstone of his philosophy.

Klein and Lucas's list of evidence is what a lawyer might call circumstantial, or "impressionistic," to use Klein and Lucas's own adjective. Taken as a whole, the documentation is either an ingenious breakthrough or a "remarkable coincidence," to quote Gavin Kennedy.[29]

A few Smithian experts have warmed up to Klein and Lucas's claim. Gavin Kennedy, who previously considered the invisible hand a "casual" metaphor, now sees a "high probability" in their thesis of deliberate centrality.[30] Others are more skeptical. "We have no direct evidence for the conjecture," states Craig Smith, an expert on Adam Smith at the University of St. Andrews. The idea that Adam Smith deliberately hid his favorite symbol of his philosophy "strikes me... as very un-Smithian," he states, and runs contrary to his policy of expressing thoughts in a "neat, plain and clever manner."[31] Placing the shorthand phrase "invisible hand" in the middle of his works may not be plain, but is it not neat and clever?

We may never know the truth, since we have no record of Smith commenting on the matter. Fortunately, one does not need to depend on the physical centrality of the "invisible hand" to recognize the doctrinal centrality of his philosophy. As Craig Smith states, "I'm not convinced that Smith deliberately placed the invisible hand at the centre of his books, but I am certain that it lies at the heart of his thinking."[32]

The Significance of the Invisible Hand Doctrine

There are many passages from the *Wealth of Nations* and *The Theory of Moral Sentiments* that elucidate the theme of "invisible hand," the idea that individuals acting in their own self-interest unwittingly benefit the public weal, or that eliminating restrictions on individuals' behaviors "better their own condition" and make society better off. Smith repeatedly advocates removal of trade barriers, state-granted privileges, and employment regulations so that entrepreneurs and enterprises can flourish.[33]

The invisible hand metaphor is an example of Smith's law of unintended consequences. Very early in *The Theory of Moral Sentiments*, Smith makes his first statement of this doctrine:

> The ancient stoics were of the opinion, that as the world was governed by the all-ruling providence of a wise, powerful, and good God, every single event ought to be regarded, as making a necessary part of the plan of the universe, and as tending to promote the general order and happiness of the

whole: that the vices and follies of mankind, therefore, made as necessary part of this plan as their wisdom and their virtue; and by that eternal art which educes good from ill, were made to tend equally to the prosperity and perfection of the great system of nature.[34]

Or this statement:

> The man of system, on the contrary, is apt to be very wise in his own conceit; and is often so enamoured with the supposed beauty of his own ideal plan of government, that he cannot suffer the smallest deviation from any part of it. He goes on to establish it completely and in all its parts, without any regard either to the great interests, or to the strong prejudices which may oppose it. He seems to imagine that he can arrange the different members of a great society with as much ease as the hand arranges the different pieces upon a chess-board. He does not consider that the pieces upon the chess-board have no other principle of motion besides that which the hand impresses upon them; but that, in the great chess-board of human society, every single piece has a principle of motion of its own, altogether different from that which the legislature might chuse to impress upon it. If those two principles coincide and act in the same direction, the game of human society will go on easily and harmoniously, and is very likely to be happy and successful. If they are opposite or different, the game will go on miserably, and the society must be at all times in the highest degree of disorder.[35]

Thus, we see how Smith's argument is comparative. To quote Klein: "Hewing to the liberty principle generally *works out better* than not doing so—in *this* respect, Arrow, Stiglitz, and Hahn *do* disfigure Smith when they identify the invisible hand with some rarified perfection. We need not rehearse Smith on the ignorance, folly, and presumption of political power, on the corruption and pathology of political ecology…. Smith sees the liberty principle as a moral, cultural, and political *focal point*, a worthy and workable principle in the otherwise dreadful fog of interventionism."[36]

To think that Adam Smith, the renowned absentminded professor, hid a little "invisible" secret in his tomes is indeed the ultimate irony. As Klein concludes, "That the phrase appears close to *the center*, and *but once*, in TMS and in WN might be taken as evidence that Smith did intend for us to take up the phrase."[37]

I find Professor Klein's story compelling, and have enjoyed showing copies of Smith's works with a bookmark in the key passages, to students, faculty, and interested friends. It has, in the words of Robert Nozick, "a certain lovely quality."[38]

Will the Real Adam Smith Please Stand Up?
My Own Odyssey

So far, I have discussed the controversies surrounding Adam Smith and the meaning and significance of his invisible hand. As an economist sympathetic with the Austrian school, I myself have gone through an odyssey in my attitude toward Adam Smith. When I first started writing my history *The Making of Modern Economics* in the late 1990s, I was still quite infatuated with everything Rothbardian, including his critique of Adam Smith. In fact, I was the one who commissioned Murray Rothbard to write his history of thought in 1980, and like everyone else, was surprised by his attack on Adam Smith. It was a shocking indictment of the Scottish philosopher celebrated by almost all free-market economists, including Rothbard's teacher Ludwig von Mises.

At that time, I had to decide, who was right, Rothbard or Mises? There was only one way to find out. I decided to read the entire 975-page *Wealth of Nations*, page by page and cover to cover, and come to my own conclusion. Two months later, I put the book down and said to myself: "Murray Rothbard is wrong and Mises is right." Adam Smith has written a grand defense of the invisible hand and economic liberalism. I followed up by reading Smith's other great work, *The Theory of Moral Sentiments* (1759), which reinforced my positive view of Smith.

My change of heart completely transformed my history. Suddenly, *The Making of Modern Economics* had a plot, a heroic figure, and a bold storyline. Adam Smith and his "system of natural liberty" became the focal point from which all economists could be judged, either adding to or distracting from his system of natural liberty. After coming under attack by socialists, Marxists, and Keynesians, the invisible hand model of Adam Smith was often left for dead but inevitably was revived, revised, and improved upon by the French, Austrian, British, and Chicago schools, and ultimately triumphed with the collapse of the socialist central-planning model in the early 1990s (although it is again being threatened by the ongoing financial crisis).

Granted, Smith made numerous mistakes in his classic work, such as his crude labor theory of value, his attack on landlords, and his failure to recognize marginal subjective values, but French, British, Austrian, and Chicago economists have done a great job improving upon the House-that-Adam-Smith-Built without destroying his fundamental system of natural liberty, and his policy prescriptions, which were largely libertarian (the classical model of limited government, free trade, balanced budgets, and sound money).

I noticed that Murray Rothbard largely ignored the strong libertarian language found in the *Wealth of Nations* and overemphasized marginal statements by Smith that were pro-government or anti-market. His attack on Smith reminds me of free-market critics who take the same parenthetical statements in Smith's writings and make him into some kind of social democrat. Both are wrong.

Here are just a few samples of Smith's strong libertarian voice in the *Wealth of Nations* (Modern Edition, 1965 [1776]):

> Every man, as long as he does not violate the laws of *justice*, is left perfectly *free* to pursue his own interest in his own way, and to bring both his industry and capital into *competition* with those of any other man, or order of men. [p. 651, emphasis added]

> To prohibit a great people…from making all that they can of every part of their own produce, or from employing their stock and industry in the way that they judge most advantageous to themselves, is a manifest violation of the most sacred rights of mankind. [p. 549]

And elsewhere:

> Little else is requisite to carry a state to the highest degree of opulence from the lowest barbarism but peace, easy taxes, and

a tolerable administration of justice; all the rest being brought about by the natural course of things. All governments which thwart the natural course are unnatural, and to support themselves, are obliged to be oppressive and tyrannical.[39]

In sum, Mises, Hayek, Friedman, and Stigler all had the right attitude when it came to Adam Smith. He established the "keystone" of the market economy.

Notes

1. George Stigler, "The Successes and Failures of Professor Smith," *Journal of Political Economy* 84:6 (December 1976): 1201. Emphasis added.
2. Milton Friedman, quoted in Fred R. Glahe, ed., *Adam Smith and the Wealth of Nations: 1776–1976 Bicentennial Essays* (Boulder, CO: Colorado Associated University Press, 1978), 7.
3. Adam Smith, *An Inquiry into the Nature and Causes of the Wealth of Nations* (Indianapolis, IN: Liberty Fund, 1981 [1776]), 456.
4. Milton and Rose Friedman, *Free to Choose* (San Diego, CA: Harcourt Brace Jovanovich, 1980), 13–14.
5. See chapter 9, "Faith and Reason in Capitalism," in Mark Skousen, *Vienna and Chicago, Friends or Foes?* (Washington, DC: Regnery, 2005) for a variety of comments, both positive and negative, about the invisible hand.
6. George J. Stigler, "The Successes and Failures of Professor Smith," *Journal of Political Economy* 84:6 (December 1976): 1201. See Stigler's quotation at the beginning of this paper.
7. George J. Stigler, "Introduction," *Selections from the Wealth of Nations* (New York: Appleton-Century-Crofts, 1957), vii–viii.
8. Ludwig von Mises, "Why Read Adam Smith Today," in Adam Smith, *The Wealth of Nations* (Washington, DC: Regnery, 1998), xi–xiii.
9. Friedrich Hayek, *The Trend of Economic Thinking: Essays on Political Economists and Economic History, The Collected Works of F. A. Hayek* (Chicago: University of Chicago Press, 1991), 119, 121.
10. Iain McLean, *Adam Smith: Radical and Egalitarian* (Edinburgh: Edinburgh University Press, 2006), 91, 120, passim, and Samuel Fleischaker, *On Adam Smith's Wealth of Nations: A Philosophical Companion* (Princeton, NJ: Princeton University Press, 2005).
11. See especially Spencer J. Pack, *Capitalism as a Moral System: Adam Smith's Critique of Free Market Economy* (London: Edward Elgar, 1991).
12. William J. Baumol and Alan S. Blinder, *Economics: Principles and Policies*, 8th ed. (Fort Worth, TX: Harcourt College Publishers, 2001), 214.
13. Frank Hahn, "Reflections on the Invisible Hand," *Lloyds Bank Review* (April 1982): 1, 4, 8.

14. See Emma Rothschild, *Economic Sentiments: Adam Smith, Condorcet, and the Enlighten-ment* (Cambridge, MA: Harvard University Press, 2001), 119; John Roemer, *Free to Lose* (Cambridge, MA: Harvard University Press, 1988), 2–3; and Frank Hahn, "Reflections on the Invisible Hand," *Lloyds Bank Review* (April 1982).

15. Alan B. Krueger, "Introduction," *The Wealth of Nations* (New York: Bantam Classics, 2003), xxiii. Krueger's recommended reading list includes works of Robert Heilbroner and Emma Rothschild, and a brief reference to an article by George Stigler.

16. Murray N. Rothbard, *Economic Thought Before Adam Smith* (London: Edward Elgar, 1995), 435–36, 448, 451, 452, and 458. Even radical economist Spencer Pack considers his attack on Smith "unduly severe" and "one of the harshest attacks every made upon Smith's work by a non-Marxist (or indeed any) economist." See "Murray Rothbard's Adam Smith," *Quarterly Journal of Austrian Economics* 1:1 (1998): 73–79.

17. Adam Smith, *An Inquiry into the Nature and Causes of the Wealth of Nations* (Indianapolis, IN: Liberty Fund, 1981 [1776]), 456.

18. Iain McLean, *Adam Smith: Radical and Egalitarian* (Edinburgh: Edinburgh University Press, 2006), 53, 82.

19. Milton Friedman, "Adam Smith's Relevance for 1976," in Fred R. Glahe, ed., *Adam Smith and the Wealth of Nations: 1776–1976 Bicentennial Essays* (Boulder, CO: Colorado Associated University Press, 1978), 17.

20. George Stigler, "The Successes and Failures of Professor Smith," *Journal of Political Economy* 84:6 (December 1976): 1201

21. Mark Skousen, *The Making of Modern Economics*, 2nd ed. (Armonk, NY: M. E. Sharpe, 2009), 219.

22. Gavin Smith, "Adam Smith and the Invisible Hand: From Metaphor to Myth," *Econ Journal Watch* 6:2 (2009): 240.

23. Emma Rothschild, *Economic Sentiments: Adam Smith, Condorcet, and the Enlightenment* (Cambridge: Harvard University Press, 2001), 116, 137.

24. Peter Minowitz, "Adam Smith's Invisible Hands," *Econ Journal Watch* 1:3 (2004): 404.

25. Daniel B. Klein, "In Adam Smith's Invisible Hands: Comment on Gavin Kennedy," *Econ Journal Watch* 6:2 (May 2009): 264–79.

26. Daniel B. Klein and Brandon Lucas, "In a Word or Two, Placed in the Middle: The Invisible Hand in Smith's Tomes," *Economic Affairs* (Institute of Economic Affairs, March 2011): 43, 50.

27. The modern Glasgow edition published by Oxford University Press and reprinted by Liberty Fund does not include the language essay, so "led by an invisible hand" is not dead-center. However, *The Theory of Moral Sentiments* published by Richard Griffin & Co. in 1854, and reprinted by Prometheus Books in 2000, does contain the language essay, and "invisible hand" appears on page 264, within five pages of the center (269).

28. Adam Smith, *Lectures on Rhetoric and Belles Lettres* (Indianapolis, IN: Liberty Fund, 1985), 95.

29. Gavin Kennedy, "Adam Smith and the Role of the Metaphor of an Invisible Hand," *Economic Affairs* (March 2011): 53. See also Gavin Smith, "Adam Smith and the Invisible Hand: From Metaphor to Myth," *Econ Journal Watch* 6:2 (May 2009): 239–63.

30. Gavin Kennedy, "Adam Smith and the Role of the Metaphor of an Invisible Hand," op. cit., 54.

31. Craig Smith, "A Comment on the Centrality of the Invisible Hand," *Economic Affairs* (March 2011): 58.

32. Ibid., 59. Ryan Hanley (Marquette University) expresses "considerable uneasiness" about Klein's thesis and is "not yet convinced." See "Another Comment on the Centrality of the Invisible Hand," *Economic Affairs* (March 2011): 60–61.

33. Adam Smith, *An Inquiry into the Nature and Causes of the Wealth of Nations* (Indianapolis, IN: Liberty Fund, 1981 [1776]), 341.

34. Adam Smith, *The Theory of Moral Sentiments* (Indianapolis, IN: Liberty Fund, 1982 [1759]), 36. For a discussion of the invisible hand as a religious symbol of the "invisible God," and the four levels of faith in capitalism, see chapter 9 in Mark Skousen, *Vienna and Chicago, Friends or Foes?* (Washington, DC: Capital Press, 2005).

35. Adam Smith, *The Theory of Moral Sentiments*, 234.

36. Daniel B. Klein, "In Adam Smith's Invisible Hands: Comment on Gavin Kennedy," *Econ Journal Watch* 6:2 (May 2009): 275.

37. Ibid., 277.

38. Robert Nozick, *Anarchy, State, and Utopia* (Oxford, UK: Basil Blackwell, 1974), 18.

39. Duguld Stewart, *Biographical Memoirs of Adam Smith* (1793).

JOHN STEELE GORDON

Wealth of a Nation:
Free Enterprise in American History

I write history and historians love coincidence. One of the best coincidences is that the most capitalist nation in the world, the United States, was born the very same year that Adam Smith published his economic masterpiece, the *Wealth of Nations*.

But no small part of the reason that the United States became the most capitalist nation was because the United States *was* new at the time of the Smithian revolution. It did not have long-established monopolies and systems of privilege to be dismantled, as European nations had. It had no immensely wealthy and powerful British East India Company or an entrenched aristocracy that dominated the country's politics. It had no ancient royal grants, such as the right to collect local tariffs,that abounded in prerevolutionary France.

Thus it was much easier for the United States to inculcate the ideas of Adam Smith into its economic system and politics than it was for the other major Western nations. This gave it immense advantages in the new economic world that was being born as the Founding Fathers met in Philadelphia to bring the United States to birth.

In *The Eighteenth Brumaire of Louis Bonaparte*, Karl Marx wrote that "Men make their own history, but they do not make it as they please; they do not make it under circumstances chosen by themselves, but

63

under circumstances directly encountered and transmitted from the past." That is certainly true, almost tautological. Marx, however, never visited the United States. (For that matter he never visited a factory—all Karl Marx knew of the proletariat he claimed to champion was what he read in books written by his fellow intellectuals. No wonder he got so much of it wrong.) Had Marx ever ventured to the New World he would have seen a country that, because of circumstances, *did* make its history as it pleased far more than any other great power.

But free enterprise had been established in the American colonies long before independence. The early settlers of America, after all, were subject to what I call the immigrant filter. Economic conditions in Britain in the early seventeenth century were bad, with much unemployment and poverty. Most people just endured. But some decided to say goodbye to everyone and everything they had ever known, risk their lives in a small boat on a vast ocean, and try to better their lot in the New World. That filter continues to this day. If America is famous for its get-up-and-go, it is because we all have ancestors who got up and came. Most of our ancestors were self-selected to be entrepreneurs.

Many of the colonies themselves were founded as profit-seeking enterprises in the brand-new business of American plantations. It was, of course, a business with a steep and expensive learning curve. Plymouth, Massachusetts Bay, and Virginia, were founded by joint-stock companies. Pennsylvania, Maryland, South Carolina, and Georgia were founded by proprietors. And while many of them wanted to build shining cities on a hill or provide a refuge for the persecuted, they all wanted to make a buck in the process. King Charles II discharged a royal debt of 16,000 pounds by granting William Penn what became the state of Pennsylvania. At nearly 30 million acres, the grant made Penn almost certainly the greatest private landowner in history.

Penn was a Quaker and he wanted to provide a refuge for his much persecuted co-religionists. He called the settlement of Pennsylvania a "Holy Experiment." But that did not mean he was indifferent to the commercial aspects of the experiment. "Though I desire to extend religious freedom," he explained, "yet I want some recompense for my troubles."

The Quaker settlers in Pennsylvania prospered mightily as did the Puritans in New England. While intensely religious in a century when religion was a far more potent force than it is today, both saw economic success as a sign of God's grace. Puritan merchants sometimes headed their ledgers with the words, "In the name of God and Profit."

The Dutch West India Company, however, had no religious interest in the New World. Its sole purpose in founding New Amsterdam was for trade. It didn't even get around to building a church for 17 years. When it finally did, it was called the Church of St. Nicholas and Santa Claus has been the occasionally inattentive patron saint of New York City ever since. Indeed, the modern Santa Claus was invented in the early nineteenth century by some New York writers, such as Washington Irving and Clement Clarke Moore.

Unlike the Massachusetts Bay Company and the Virginia Company, the Dutch West India Company made a profit in its very first year in New Amsterdam. The Dutch had the most advanced financial system and the most market-oriented economy in Europe at this time and, not coincidentally, were rapidly becoming the richest nation in Europe. Simon Schama aptly titled his book of this period in Dutch history *An Embarrassment of Riches*.

The Dutch brought this enterprising spirit with them to the New World, along with the religious tolerance that was their hallmark. When Governor Peter Stuyvesant, a sincere member of the Calvinist Dutch Reformed Church, tried to expel the Quakers and Jews from New Amsterdam, they appealed to the Company in the Netherlands in a the Flushing Remonstrance. The company quickly wrote Governor Stuyvesant, and told him in no uncertain terms to mind his own damn business so that the Quakers and the Jews could mind theirs.

As early as the 1640s, while its population was still under a thousand, the little city at the tip of Manhattan Island was the most cosmopolitan in North America, as it has been ever since. A French priest counted no fewer than eighteen languages being spoken on the streets in that decade. Even today, deep within the heart of the vast metropolis that is New York City, there lives still—like the child within the man—that little, hustly-bustly, let's-make-a-deal Dutch village. And the making of money is still the city's dearest love.

Nothing could make the Dutch approach to New World settlement clearer than the seal of New Netherlands: a beaver encircled with wampum. Wampum, the form of money used by the Indians, is a tubular bead made from clamshells, usually strung with others in intricate patterns. And wampum played an important part in the early history of what would become the greatest city in the Western hemisphere and the financial capital of the world.

When the city was only forty years old and Wall Street was not its financial center but its northern defensive boundary, Frederick Philipse cornered the wampum market. Born in Holland in 1626, he came with his father to New Amsterdam in 1647. Trained as a carpenter, in 1652 Philipse actually helped build the wall that gave Wall Street its name. He did not remain a carpenter for long, however. Capable and ambitious, he soon took one of the royal roads to wealth: He married a rich widow. With his wife's money behind him, Philipse began to trade with the Indians.

The Indians, the source of the furs that were the mainstay of New York's economy in the seventeenth century, did not want gold or silver in payment. They wanted what they regarded as real money: wampum. In 1650 six white beads or three black beads were worth one stuiver, the Dutch equivalent of a nickel.

Unfortunately, wampum inflation set in, and by 1659 it took sixteen white beads to equal a stuiver. This played havoc with the local economy, not only because it drove up the cost of furs but because the settlers as well as the Indians used wampum in day-to-day transactions. Governor Stuyvesant tried the usual government remedy (price controls) with the usual results (they were ignored).

Then Frederick Philipse began buying wampum and taking it out of circulation by burying it in hogsheads in his backyard. He soon controlled the wampum market and succeeded in raising its price dramatically. By 1666 it took only three white beads to equal a stuiver.

The concept of a central bank would not even exist until the eighteenth century, but in the middle of the seventeenth century Frederick Philipse was, in effect, acting as one, regulating the money supply and doubtless making a tidy profit in the process, as central banks usually do. He went on to become the colony's richest citizen, marrying a second rich widow along the way, with trading interests as distant as the East Indies and Madagascar.

Wampum would remain a regular part of the money supply in some of the American colonies until the mid-eighteenth century. Then, a man in

New Jersey, imbued with the spirt of free enterprise, invented a wampum counterfeiting machine and destroyed the value of the real thing.

By that time the American economy was the richest on earth, at least on a per-capita basis. While firm economic statistics for the eighteenth century are hard to come by, consider this. The soldiers in the Continental Army averaged two inches taller than those fighting in the British army (and who were often their close relations). The Americans simply had a much better diet as children than their British cousins.

By that time, the American colonies had the second-largest merchant marine in the world, after Britain, with the second-largest shipbuilding industry. They were producing one-seventh of the world's pig iron as well as exporting large quantities of agricultural produce.

Britain, which had gone deeply into debt during the French and Indian war, woke up to the growing economic power of its colonies and, therefore, their ability to pay taxes. While it accurately estimated the Americans' ability to pay taxes, unfortunately for Britain it badly overestimated the Americans' willingness to pay them. The result was the American Revolution.

Once the Constitution was written and adopted, the American economy began to expand rapidly. That was due partly to a rapidly growing population and, to no small degree, to the financial system put in place by Alexander Hamilton that established for the first time in American history a coherent money supply and marketable bonds that could serve as collateral for loans.

But the Constitution also put in place several provisions that would allow free enterprise to flourish. It forbade states to coin money, make anything but gold or silver legal tender, impair the obligation of contract, or lay duties on exports or imports. Exports could not be taxed by the federal government. No port could be given preference over another, nor could interstate shipping be required to enter any port or pay duties there. It made admiralty law and bankruptcy a federal responsibility, so that bankrupts could not escape their creditors merely by moving to another state.

Most important, it gave Congress the power to regulate interstate commerce. But it was not clear exactly what that meant—until 1824, when the Supreme Court explained it in what the great historian of the court, Charles Warren, called "the Emancipation Proclamation of the American Economy."

New York state had granted a monopoly of steamboat navigation to Robert Fulton and Robert Livingston after Fulton had successfully sailed a steamboat from New York to Albany within the requisite time period. The Territory of Louisiana, whose governor, most conveniently, was Livingston's brother, did the same. The monopoly of steamboating in New York waters lasted far longer than it did in New Orleans and would have far greater consequences.

New Jersey and Connecticut retaliated as best they could by banning New York boats from their waters as theirs were banned from New York's. One man from New Jersey, Thomas Gibbons, decided to fight both in court and in the marketplace. He owned a steamboat named the *Stoudinger* (although, because it was very small, it was usually known as the *Mouse*), which he put on the New York–New Brunswick run, the first leg of the quickest route to Philadelphia. He hired as its captain a young man from Staten Island named Cornelius Vanderbilt.

Vanderbilt, still in his twenties, had already owned a small fleet of sailing ships, but he realized that the future belonged to steam and went to work for Gibbons to gain experience and build up his capital so that he could go into steamboats himself. He soon convinced Gibbons to build a larger boat, designed by Vanderbilt, which Gibbons named the *Bellona*, after the Roman goddess of war. In that far more classically oriented age, the implication in the name was clear to everyone.

Flying a flag that read "New Jersey Must Be Free!," Vanderbilt would steam boldly to New York, dock wherever the New York state authorities trying to arrest him seemed not to be, and immediately disappear into the city. The authorities didn't dare seize the boat itself, knowing that New Jersey would retaliate by seizing the first monopoly steamboat it could lay its hands on. At sailing time he would sneak back as near to the ship as possible and then make a dash for it, the crew casting off the instant he was aboard. The monopoly even tried to buy Vanderbilt by offering him the colossal salary of $5,000 a year, but he declined abruptly.

While the monopoly was having limited success preventing competition in the real world, it not surprisingly kept beating Gibbons in the New York state courts. After five years the case finally reached the United States Supreme Court, and Gibbons hired two of the best lawyers in the country to represent him there: Daniel Webster, then serving as a congressman from Massachusetts, and William Wirt, who was Attorney General of the United States, although acting here in a private capacity.

Webster took an entire day to deliver what was universally recognized as a brilliant legal oration. William Wirt and the lawyers for the Livingston interests also spoke eloquently and at length. The decision was widely awaited, not only in New York but elsewhere as well.

The opinion was read by Chief Justice John Marshall on March 2, only three weeks after hearing arguments. "Commerce undoubtedly is traffic," Marshall wrote for a unanimous court, "but it is something more, it is intercourse," and it ". . . is regulated by prescribing rules for carrying on that intercourse." Since the Constitution gave the federal government the power to regulate interstate commerce, the federal government and the federal government alone, wrote Marshall, was empowered to prescribe the rules.

This is precisely what Webster had argued (patting himself on the back as usual, Webster wrote that "The opinion of the Court, as rendered by the Chief Justice, was little else than a recital of my argument.") But it was also a new and breathtaking assertion of federal power. President Monroe, in a veto message to Congress in 1822, had written that the power granted by the Constitution to regulate interstate commerce did not extend beyond the power to lay duties on foreign commerce and to prevent duties being laid on trade between the states, powers already explicitly in the Constitution.

President Monroe, in other words, thought the Interstate Commerce Clause to be basically a nullity. *Gibbons v. Ogden* made it one of the federal government's greatest powers, one that has often been abused in recent years. In 1995 Congress actually tried to ban handguns within 1,000 feet of a school, basing the law on its power to regulate the interstate commerce in handguns. The Supreme Court, in one of its rare recent decisions that limits the commerce power, threw out the law, saying that this was obviously an exercise of the police power reserved to the states, not a commercial regulation.

The *Gibbons* decision was greeted jubilantly everywhere, and many newspapers reprinted the decision in its entirety. The economic effects were immediate. Fares from New Haven to New York, for instance, fell by 40 percent thanks to competition, and the number of steamboats operating in New York waters jumped from six to forty-three in less than two years. By 1850 Cornelius Vanderbilt, then known by his still-familiar soubriquet of "the Commodore," was the largest steamboat owner in the country.

But the long-term effects were even more profound. States stopped granting monopolies of any sort to rent-seeking influential citizens, as all monopolies were now presumptively unconstitutional. Other barriers to interstate commerce, erected for parochial benefit, fell as well. In other words, *Gibbons v. Ogden* was a mortal blow to the crony capitalism of the day. But crony capitalism is always a clear and present danger to free enterprise. Just ask the bondholders of General Motors who were shunted aside for the benefit of the United Auto Workers.

Thanks to *Gibbons v. Ogden*, the United States became the world's largest truly common market, just as the power of steam to move goods cheaply over long distances—a power merely hinted at by the steamboat—was about to grow exponentially. The railroad would prove the seminal invention of the nineteenth century and would create the modern economy for which *Gibbons v. Ogden* had readied the United States.

By the time of the Civil War, the United States had one of the largest economies in the world and the war greatly enlarged it further. Because of the war, the industrialization of the American economy, already well underway, expanded greatly. In 1859 there had been 140,000 manufacturing firms in the United States. A decade later there were 252,000. The domestic production of iron railroad rails—a good measure of industrial might in the mid-nineteenth century—went from 205,000 tons in 1860 to 620,000 tons in 1870, more than a threefold increase. But industries less central to the economy were also boosted by the war. The process patented by Gail Borden in 1856 for canning condensed milk saw a great increase in demand, which helped spark a boom in the food processing industry.

Wall Street also prospered, almost beyond calculation, in the Civil War years. Although the outbreak of the war caused panic, as the sudden onset of a great war always does, it was soon clear that the business of the Street—the trading of securities—would greatly increase. As the national debt soared by a factor of forty, bond trading soared equally. More, it was clear that much of the money the government was spending would go to firms such as iron mills, gun foundries, railroads, telegraph companies, and textile and shoe manufacturers. The profits of these firms would be invested in Wall Street and their capital needs met by it.

Wall Street quickly blossomed into the one of the largest securities market on earth, second only to London. Fortunes were made in the next few years. In 1864, J. P. Morgan, only twenty-seven years old, had a taxable income of $53,287, fifty times what a skilled worker might expect to earn in a year.

Somewhat paradoxically, it was the Armageddon of the Civil War, with all its cost in blood and treasure, that brought a new economic dynamism into being in the United States. The very size of the struggle induced a solemn and profound pride in what had been saved thereby: the American Union.

The Civil War transformed the United States (a phrase that had, before the war, been grammatically construed in the plural—the United States "are") from a collection of associated states into a nation, one whose name was construed in the singular—the United States "is." The ancient motto of the country, *e pluribus unum*, had been achieved, at the cost of 600,000 dead. Among the great powers today, only ethnically homogeneous Japan has fewer centrifugal forces at work in its body politic than the multi-ethnic United States.

Salmon P. Chase, the Secretary of the Treasury for much of the war, felt this new attitude as early as 1863. "We began without capital," he wrote that year, "and if we should lose the *greater* part of it before this [war] is over, labor will bring it back again and with a power hitherto unfelt among us."

The fact that the war had been financed internally, and with such vast sums, brought home just how rich and powerful the nation had become. America is "to-day the most powerful nation on the face of the globe," Congressman Godlove S. Orth told an audience in Lafayette, Indiana, in 1864. "This war has been the means of developing resources and capabilities such as you never before dreamed that you possessed."

The people knew what they possessed now, and, with the end of the Civil War, as the country's military forces shrank quickly to insignificance, they would, in the next three decades, use those new resources and capabilities to astonish the world as they pursued their self-interests in the country's free enterprise system.

Although already a major industrial power, in 1865 the country was still basically an agricultural one. Not a single industrial concern was listed on the New York Stock Exchange. By the turn of the twentieth century, a mere generation later, the United States had the largest and most modern industrial economy on earth, one characterized by giant corporations undreamed of in 1865. An importer of capital since its earliest days, the United States had become a world financial power as well, the equal of Great Britain.

In 1860, the U.S. imported nearly all its steel. By 1900, the American steel industry was larger than that of Great Britain and Germany combined, and it was exporting steel to both those countries. The greatest steelmaker of the day, Andrew Carnegie, had started as a penniless immigrant from Scotland. When he sold out to J. P. Morgan in 1901 he was, in Morgan's words, "the richest man in the world."

The need to devise rules and institutions that would allow this new economy to flourish, and to assure that its fruits were equitably enjoyed by all segments of society, would dominate American domestic politics for the next century, just as preserving the Union and slavery had dominated the politics of the antebellum period.

Free enterprise has never meant unregulated enterprise. In unregulated markets the temptation to cheat is far too great. Welcome to human nature. Imagine what the Super Bowl would turn into if those guys in the stripe shirts weren't on the field. Of course, in the game of the free market, the guys in striped shirts have a bad habit of coming up with more and more rules—ever more rules being in *their* self-interest.

These rules can be not only excessive, but corrupted as well. The environmental regulations put into place in the last forty years, for instance, have now become a prime means for self-described "environmentalists," who are in reality anti-capitalists, to stymie economic projects. Their lawyers have learned how to game the legal system in order, not to find justice, but to endlessly delay these projects.

Many of the devices adopted to govern the new economy in the late nineteenth century would come through governmental and legislative action, especially in the latter decades. But, in fact, just as many would emerge from the private sector, as lawyers, bankers, brokers, railroaders, labor leaders, and industrialists sought to advance their own long-term self-interests. Bar associations, for instance, were established at this time to govern the conduct of lawyers, a group always in need of governance.

It was, in short, a typically messy democratic process, but, as is usual with democratic processes, it worked in the long term. No society in history had ever needed to govern a highly dynamic industrially based economy in a nation that was constitutionally a federal republic of limited powers. The United States learned how to do so, using, largely unconsciously, the great insights of the Founding Fathers: that men are not angels, that they are driven by self-interest, and, as Adam Smith had demonstrated, that this self-interest could be exploited for the general good.

Although sometimes wracked by severe depressions, the American economy flourished abundantly over the next 140 years precisely because the nation had devised a highly effective system of checks and balances for governing that economy in the decades after the Civil War.

Immediately after the war, however, nothing characterized American politics, and thus the American economy, so much as corruption. There were, in effect, no men in striped shirts on the field, and the result, for a few years, was capitalism red in tooth and claw. It was often entertaining, at least for those who were not directly involved, but it was no way to run an economy. Capitalism without regulation and regulators is inherently unstable, as people usually put their short-term self-interests ahead of the interests of the system as a whole, and either chaos or plutocracy will result.

As Herbert Hoover explained, "The trouble with capitalism is capitalists."

Wall Street, in particular perhaps, was almost totally unregulated. There were several exchanges in operation at the end of the Civil War and none of them had the power to control the speculators. Neither did the courts, for they were utterly corrupt. "The [New York] Supreme Court is our *Cloaca Maxima*, with lawyers for its rats" George Templeton Strong, a very successful lawyer himself wrote in his diary. In 1868, the popular English *Fraser's Magazine* wrote that "in New York there is a custom among litigants as peculiar to that city, it is to be hoped, as it is supreme within it, of retaining a judge as well as a lawyer." In 1868, the New York state legislature actually passed a bill that in effect, if not in so many words, legalized bribery.

Only when the two largest exchanges, the Open Board of Brokers and the New York Stock Exchange, merged in 1869 did Wall Street's wild-west days end. The new exchange was now powerful enough to enforce rules. They required members to trade listed securities only, where the exchange could keep an eye on things. Listed companies had to maintain an open registry of securities and give advance notice of new issues. Wall Street—while still no place for fools, and it never will be—was now a well-regulated financial market, about 30 percent the size of London's. By 1900 it would be London's equal.

The great Wall Street banks that were emerging in the 1880s, such as J. P. Morgan & Co. and Kuhn Loeb, and the New York Stock Exchange began demanding two vital new ways of doing business. Listed firms, and those hoping to raise capital through the banks, were required to keep their books according to what became known as generally accepted accounting principles (GAAP).

There are many ways to keep honest books—and an infinite number of ways to keep dishonest ones—so it is important that all companies keep them the same way, so that they can be compared. Second, they were required to have their books certified as honest and complete by independent accountants. It was at this time that accountancy became an independent, self-governing profession, like law and medicine.

Today, the ideas of consistent bookkeeping according to a fixed set of rules and independent certification are so obviously good ideas that no one even thinks of challenging them. Indeed there is only one major area of American life where they are not practiced: government. No small part of the reason that the federal government and many state governments are in financial crisis is that they are able to cook their books and often do so with a vengeance. Nothing would rein in the power of government quicker or more strongly than to impose the equivalent of generally accepted accounting principles and independent certification of government books.

By 1900, the United States had the world's largest economy, thanks to its devotion to free enterprise and its inherent economic advantages, and the world's highest standard of living. The two world wars would turn it into the most powerful country the world has ever known, both in absolute terms and relative to the other great powers. In 1945, with the other powers financially and often physically devastated by World War II, the United States had about half of the world's GDP. Even today, with other countries economically recovered—often with massive American help, perhaps the greatest instance of enlightened self-interest ever—and China growing at an extraordinary rate, the United States still has about a quarter of world GDP.

But we are now in a new world. The steam engine—with its ability to input vast amounts of low-cost, work-performing energy into the economy—overturned the agriculturally based economy of the eighteenth century. Thereby, it overturned the social and political structures that had been based on that economy.

Today, the microprocessor is rapidly overturning the industrially based economy of the late-nineteenth and twentieth centuries. The microprocessor can input at very low cost the storage, retrieval, and, crucially, the manipulation of information into the economy. Like the invention of movable type 500 years ago, the microprocessor has lowered the cost of information by orders of magnitude.

The regulatory apparatus put in place to govern an industrially based economy is now increasingly antique and obsolete in a knowledge-based economy. More, the old regulatory apparatus is often used for political, not regulatory, purposes.

Consider antitrust. First passed in the late nineteenth century, it became a powerful—many would say too powerful—tool in the early twentieth century to prevent overweening corporate power. By the late twentieth century it was showing signs of irrelevance in a world where the pace of economic change was accelerating sharply. When the anti-trust prosecution of IBM began in 1969, for instance, IBM was utterly dominant in the computer industry, which was then characterized by mainframe computers. The case was finally abandoned by the government in 1983, when IBM was already spiraling downward in the new personal-computer world made possible by the microprocessor.

But antitrust is a very handy weapon for a basically antibusiness administration—I won't mention any names—to use to bludgeon companies into following the administration's wishes.

Likewise, unions, which once were important to make sure that the balance between labor and capital was equitable, are now economic dinosaurs. Union membership peaked nearly sixty years ago, at 35 percent of the workforce. Today, in the private sector, it is down to about 7 percent, as unskilled and low-skilled jobs disappear. Only in the public sector—where unions should never have been allowed in the first place—is the union movement growing.

But out-of-date laws such as the Wagner Act of 1935 give unions far more political power than their economic power and utility justify. Just ask Governor Scott Walker of Wisconsin.

As in the late nineteenth century, there will be formidable political battles ahead in order to bring the new economy and the regulatory structure needed to govern that economy into sync.

My fellow political junkies are going to have a field day.

But the American people remain both the most democratic and the most entrepreneurial on earth. Just as Frederick Philipse did in the seventeenth century, Andrew Carnegie in the nineteenth, Henry Ford in the twentieth, and Steve Jobs in the twenty-first centuries, the Americans of tomorrow will find ways, by pursuing their self-interests, to enrich the world as they prosper mightily in their nation's economy. For three hundred years that economy has been the wonder of the world thanks to Americans' devotion to free enterprise.

LUDWIG VON MISES

WHY READ ADAM SMITH TODAY?

A popular legend calls Adam Smith the Father of Political Economy and his two great books—*The Theory of Moral Sentiments*, first published in 1759, and *An Inquiry into the Nature and Causes of the Wealth of Nations*, first published in 1776—epoch-making in economic history as well as in the evolution of economic thought. However, this is not quite correct. Smith did not inaugurate a new chapter in social philosophy and did not sow on land hitherto left uncultivated. His books were rather the consummation, summarization, and perfection of lines of thought developed by eminent authors—mostly British—over a period of more than a hundred years. Smith's books did not lay the foundation stone, but the keystone, of a marvelous system of ideas. Their eminence is to be seen precisely in the fact that they integrated the main body of these ideas into a systematic whole. They presented the essence of the ideology of freedom, individualism, and prosperity, with admirable logical clarity and in an impeccable literary form.

Ludwig von Mises, *Economic Freedom and Interventionism: An Anthology of Articles and Essays*, edited by Bettina Bien Greaves (Indianapolis, IN: Liberty Fund, 2006), 133–35. See also the Ludwig von Mises Institute—http://mises.org/efandi/ch24.asp. Introduction to the 1953 Regnery edition of Adam Smith, *An Inquiry into the Nature and Causes of the Wealth of Nations.* Reprinted by permission of Bettina Bien Greaves.

It was this ideology that blew up the institutional barriers to the display of the individual citizen's initiative and thereby to economic improvement. It paved the way for the unprecedented achievements of laissez-faire capitalism. The practical application of liberal principles multiplied population figures and, in the countries committed to the policies of economic freedom, secured even to less capable and less industrious people a standard of living higher than that of the well-to-do of the "good old" days. The average American wage-earner would not like to dwell in the dirty, badly lighted, and poorly heated palatial houses, in which the members of the privileged English and French aristocracy lived 200 years ago, or to do without those products of capitalist big business that render his life comfortable.

The ideas that found their classical expression in the two books of Adam Smith demolished the traditional philosophy of Mercantilism and opened the way for capitalist mass production for the needs of the masses. Under capitalism the common man is the much-talked-about customer who "is always right." His buying makes efficient entrepreneurs rich, and his abstention from buying forces inefficient entrepreneurs to go out of business. Consumers' sovereignty, which is the characteristic mark of business in a free world, is the signature of production activities in the countries of Western Civilization.

The civilization is today furiously attacked by Eastern barbarians from without and by domestic self-styled Progressives from within. Their aim is, as one of their intellectual leaders, the Frenchman Georges Sorel,* put it, to destroy what exists. They want to substitute central planning by the government for the autonomy of the individual citizens, and totalitarianism for democracy. As their muddy and unwarranted schemes cannot stand the criticism leveled by sound economics, they exult in smearing and calumniating all their opponents.

Adam Smith too is a target of these smear campaigns. One of the most passionate advocates of destructionism had the nerve to call him, in the Introduction to an inexpensive edition of the *Wealth of Nations*, "an unconscious mercenary in the service of a rising capitalist class" and to add that "he gave a new dignity to greed and a new

---

* Georges Sorel (1847–1922), a French political thinker, advocated at various times in his life violence, Marxism, revolutionary syndicalism, and Bolshevism.

sanctification to the predatory impulses."[1] Other leftists resort to even still ruder insults.

As against such shallow opinions it may be appropriate to quote the verdict of wiser judges. The British historian Henry Thomas Buckle (1821–1862), declared "that this solitary Scotchman has, by the publication of one single work, contributed more toward the happiness of man than has been effected by the united abilities of all the statesmen and legislators of whom history has presented an authentic record." The English economist Walter Bagehot (1826–1877) said about the *Wealth of Nations*: "The life of almost everyone in England—perhaps of everyone—is different and better in consequence of it."

A work that has been praised in such a way by eminent authors must not be left on the shelves of libraries for the perusal of specialists and historians only. At least its most important chapters should be read by all those who are eager to learn something about the past. There can hardly be found another book that could initiate a man better into the study of the history of modern ideas and the prosperity created by industrialization. Its publication date—1776, the year of the American Declaration of Independence—marks the dawn of freedom both political and economic. There is no Western nation that was not benefited by policies inspired by the ideas that received their classical formulation in this unique treatise.

However, a warning must be given. Nobody should believe that he will find in Smith's *Wealth of Nations* information about present-day economics or about present-day problems of economic policy. Reading Smith is no more a substitute for studying economics than reading Euclid is a substitute for the study of mathematics. It is at best an historical introduction into the study of modern ideas and policies. Neither will the reader find in the *Wealth of Nations* a refutation of the teachings of Marx, Veblen, Keynes, and their followers. It is one of the tricks of the socialists to make people believe that there are no other writings recommending economic freedom than those of 18th-century authors and that in their, of course unsuccessful, attempts to refute Smith they have done all that is needed to prove the correctness of

---

[1] Max Lerner in the Modern Library edition of the *Wealth of Nations* (New York: Random House, 1937), p. ix.

their own point of view. Socialist professors—not only in the countries behind the Iron Curtain—withheld from their students any knowledge about the existence of contemporary economists who deal with the problems concerned in an unbiased scientific way and who have devastatingly exploded the spurious schemes of all brands of socialism and interventionism. If they are blamed for their partiality, they protest their innocence, "Did we not read in class some chapters of Adam Smith?" they retort. In their pedagogy the reading of Smith serves as a blind for ignoring all sound contemporary economics.

Read the great book of Smith. But don't think that this may save you the trouble of seriously studying modern economic books. Smith sapped the prestige of 18th-century government controls. He does not say anything about the controls of 1952 or the Communist challenge.

LUDWIG VON MISES

THE HARMONY OF THE "RIGHTLY UNDERSTOOD" INTERESTS

From time immemorial men have prattled about the blissful conditions their ancestors enjoyed in the original "state of nature." From old myths, fables, and poems the image of this primitive happiness passed into many popular philosophies of the seventeenth and eighteenth centuries. In their language the term *natural* denoted what was good and beneficial in human affairs, while the term *civilization* had the connotation of opprobrium. The fall of man was seen in the deviation from the primitive conditions of ages in which there was but little deference between man and other animals. At that time, these romantic eulogists of the past asserted, there were no conflicts between men. Peace was undisturbed in the Garden of Eden.

Yet nature does not generate peace and good will. The characteristic mark of the "state of nature" is irreconcilable conflict. Each specimen is the rival of all other specimens. The means of subsistence are scarce and do not grant survival to all. The conflicts can never disappear. If a band of men, united with the object of defeating rival bands, succeeds

Ludwig von Mises, *Human Action: A Treatise on Economics*, 4th revised edition (San Francisco, CA: Fox & Wilkes, 1996), 673–82. See also the Ludwig von Mises Institute—http://mises.org/Books/humanaction.pdf.

in annihilating its foes, new antagonisms arise among the victors over the distribution of the booty. The source of the conflicts is always the fact that each man's portion curtails the portions of all other men.

What makes friendly relations between human beings possible is the higher productivity of the division of labor. It removes the natural conflict of interests. For where there is division of labor, there is no longer question of the distribution of a supply not capable of enlargement. Thanks to the higher productivity of labor performed under the division of tasks, the supply of goods multiplies. A pre-eminent common interest, the preservation and further intensification of social cooperation, becomes paramount and obliterates all essential collisions. Catallactic competition is substituted for biological competition. It makes for harmony of the interests of all members of society. The very condition from which the irreconcilable conflicts of biological competition arise—viz., the fact that all people by and large strive after the same things—is transformed into a factor making for harmony of interests. Because many people or even all people want bread, clothes, shoes, and cars, large-scale production of these goods becomes feasible and reduces the costs of production to such an extent that they are accessible at low prices. The fact that my fellow man wants to acquire shoes as I do, does not make it harder for me to get shoes, but easier. What enhances the price of shoes is the fact that nature does not provide a more ample supply of leather and other raw material required, and that one must submit to the disutility of labor in order to transform these raw materials into shoes. The catallactic competition of those who, like me, are eager to have shoes makes shoes cheaper, not more expensive.

This is the meaning of the theorem of the harmony of the rightly understood interests of all members of the market society.[1] When the classical economists made this statement, they were trying to stress two points: First, that everybody is interested in the preservation of the social division of labor, the system that multiplies the productivity of human efforts. Second, that in the market society consumers' demand ultimately directs all production activities. The fact that not all human wants can be satisfied is not due to inappropriate social institutions or to deficiencies of the system of the market economy. It is a natural

---

[1] For "rightly understood" interests we may as well say interests "in the long run."

condition of human life. The belief that nature bestows upon man inexhaustible riches and that misery is an outgrowth of man's failure to organize the good society is entirely fallacious. The "state of nature" which the reformers and utopians depicted as paradisiac was in fact a state of extreme poverty and distress. "Poverty," says Bentham, "is not the work of the laws, it is the primitive condition of the human race."[2] Even those at the base of the social pyramid are much better off than they would have been in the absence of social cooperation. They too are benefitted by the operation of the market economy and participate in the advantages of civilized society.

The nineteenth-century reformers did not drop the cherished fable of the original earthly paradise. Frederick Engels incorporated it in the Marxian account of mankind's social evolution. However, they no longer set up the bliss of the *aureau aetas* as a pattern for social and economic reconstruction. They contrast the alleged depravity of capitalism with the ideal happiness man will enjoy in the socialist Elysium of the future. The socialist mode of production will abolish the fetters by means of which capitalism checks the development of the productive forces, and will increase the productivity of labor and wealth beyond all measure. The preservation of free enterprise and the private ownership of the means of production benefits exclusively the small minority of parasitic exploiters and harms the immense majority of working men. Hence there prevails within the frame of the market society an irreconcilable conflict between the interests of "capital" and those of "labor." This class struggle can disappear only when a fair system of social organization—either socialism or interventionism—is substituted for the manifestly unfair capitalist mode of production.

Such is the almost universally accepted social philosophy of our age. It was not created by Marx, although it owes its popularity mainly to the writings of Marx and the Marxians, but no less by most of those parties who emphatically declare their anti-Marxism and pay lip service to free enterprise. It is the official social philosophy of Roman Catholicism as well as of Anglo-Catholicism; it is supported by many eminent champions of the various Protestant denominations and of the Orthodox Oriental Church. It is an essential part of the teachings

---

[2] Cf. Bentham, *Principles of the Civil Code*, in "Works," I, 309.

of Italian Fascism and of German Nazism and of all varieties of interventionist doctrines. It was the ideology of the Sozialpolitik of the Hohenzollerns in Germany and of the French royalists aiming at the restoration of the house of Bourbon-Orleans, of the New Deal of President Roosevelt, and of the nationalists of Asia and Latin America. The antagonisms between these parties and factions refer to accidental issues—such as religious dogma, constitutional institutions, foreign policy—and, first of all, to the characteristic features of the social system that is to be substituted for capitalism. But they all agree in the fundamental thesis that the very existence of the capitalist system harms the vital interests of the immense majority of workers, artisans, and small farmers, and they all ask in the name of social justice for the abolition of capitalism.[3]

All socialist and interventionist authors and politicians base their analysis and critique of the market economy on two fundamental errors. First, they fail to recognize the speculative character inherent in all endeavors to provide for future want-satisfaction, i.e., in all human action. They naively assume that there cannot exist any doubt about the measures to be applied for the best possible provisioning of the

---

[3] The official doctrine of the Roman Church is outlined in the encyclical *Quadragismo anno* of Pope Pius XI (1931). The Anglo-Catholic doctrine is presented by the late William Temple, Archbishop of Canterbury, in the book *Christianity and the Social Order* (Penguin Special, 1942). Representative of the ideas of European continental Protestantism is the book of Emil Brunner, *Justice and the Social Order*, trans. by M. Hottinger (New York, 1945). A highly significant document is the section on "The Church and Disorder of Society" of the draft report which the World Council of Churches in September, 1948, recommended for appropriate action to the one hundred and fifty odd denominations whose delegates are members of the Council. For the ideas of Nicolas Berdyawe, the most eminent apologist of Russian Orthodoxy, cf. his book *The Origin of Russian Communism* (London, 1937), especially pp. 217–218 and 225. It is often asserted that an essential difference between the Marxians and the other socialist and interventionist parties is to be found in the fact that the Marxians stand for class struggle, while the latter parties look at the class struggle as upon a deplorable outgrowth of the irreconcilable conflict of class interest inherent in capitalism and want to overcome it by the realization of the reforms they recommend. However, the Marxians do not praise and kindle the class struggle for its own sake. In their eyes, the class struggle is good only because it is the device by means of which the "productive forces," those mysterious forces directing the course of human evolution, are bound to bring about the "classless" society in which there will be neither classes nor class conflicts.

consumers. In a socialist commonwealth there will be no need for the production tsar (or the central board of production management) to speculate. He will "simply" have to resort to those measures which are beneficial to his wards. The advocates of a planned economy have never conceived that the problem is to allocate scarce factors of production in the various branches of production in such a way that no wants considered more urgent should remain unsatisfied because the factors of production required for their satisfaction were employed, i.e., wasted, for the satisfaction of wants considered less urgent. This economic problem must not be confused with the technological problem. Technological knowledge can merely tell us what could be achieved under the present state of our scientific insight. It does not answer the questions as to what should be produced and in what quantities, and which of the multitude of technological processes available should be chosen. Deluded by their failure to grasp this essential matter, the advocates of a planned society believe that the production tsar will never err in his decisions. In the market economy the entrepreneurs and capitalists cannot avoid committing serious blunders because they know neither what the consumers want nor what their competitors are doing. The general manager of a socialist state will be infallible because he alone will have the power to determine what should be produced and how, and because no action of other people will cross his plans.[4]

The second fundamental error involved in the socialists' critique of the market economy stems from their faulty theory of wages. They have failed to realize that wages are the price paid for the earner's achievement, i.e., for the contribution of his efforts to the processing of the good concerned or, as people say, for the value which his services add to the value of the materials. No matter whether there are time wages or piecework wages, the employer always buys the worker's performance and services, not his time. It is therefore not true that in the unhampered market economy the worker has no personal interest in the execution of his task. The socialists are badly mistaken in asserting that those paid a certain rate per hour, per day, per week, per month, or per year are not impelled by their own selfish interests when they work

---

[4] The thorough exposure of this delusion is provided by the proof of the impossibility of economic calculation under socialism. See below the fifth part of this book.

efficiently. It is not lofty ideals and the sense of duty that deter a worker paid according to the length of time worked from carelessness and loafing around the shop, but very substantial arguments. He who works more and better gets higher pay, and he who wants to earn more must increase the quantity and improve the quality of his performance. The hard-boiled employers are not so gullible as to let themselves be cheated by slothful employees; they are not so negligent as those governments who pay salaries to hosts of loafing bureaucrats. Neither are the wage earners so stupid as not to know that laziness and inefficiency are heavily penalized on the labor market.[5]

On the shaky ground of their misconception of the catallactic nature of wages, the socialist authors have advanced fantastic fables about the increase in the productivity of labor to be expected from realization of their plans. Under capitalism, they say, the worker's zeal is seriously impaired because he is aware of the fact that he himself does not reap the fruits of his labor and that his toil and trouble enrich his employer, this parasitic and idle exploiter. But under socialism every worker will know that he works for the benefit of society, of which he himself is a part. This knowledge will provide him with the most powerful incentive to do his best. An enormous increase in the productivity of labor and thereby in wealth will result.

However, the identification of the interests of each worker and those of the socialist commonwealth is a purely legalistic and formalistic fiction which has nothing to do with the real state of affairs. While the sacrifices an individual worker makes in intensifying his own exertion burden him alone, only an infinitesimal fraction of the produce of his additional exertion benefits himself and improves his own well-being. While the individual worker enjoys completely the pleasures he may reap by yielding to the temptation to carelesness and laziness, the resulting impairment of the social dividend curtails his own share only infinitesimally. Under such a socialist mode of production all personal incentives which selfishness provides under capitalism are removed, and a premium is put upon laziness and negligence. Whereas in a capitalist society selfishness incites everyone to the utmost diligence, in a socialist society it makes for inertia and laxity. The socialists may still

---

[5] Cf. above, pp. 600–602.

babble about the miraculous change in human nature that the advent
of socialism will effect, and about the substitution of lofty altruism for
mean egotism. But they must no longer indulge in fables about the
marvelous effects the selfishness of each individual will bring about
under socialism.[6]

No judicious man can fail to conclude from the evidence of these
considerations that in the market economy the productivity of labor
is incomparably higher than it would be under socialism. However,
this cognition does not settle the question between the advocates of
capitalism and those of socialism from a praxeological, i.e., scientific,
point of view.

A bona fide advocate of socialism who is free from bigotry,
prepossession, and malice could still contend: "It may be true that
P, the total net income turned out in a market society, is larger than
p, the total net income turned out in a socialist society. But if the
socialist system assigns to each of its members an equal share of p (viz.
$p/z = d$), all those whose income in the market society is smaller than d
are favored by the substitution of socialism for capitalism. It may happen
that this group of people includes the majority of men. At any rate it
becomes evident that the doctrine of the harmony between the rightly
understood interests of all members of the market society is untenable.
There is a class of men whose interests are hurt by the very existence
of the market economy and who would be better off under socialism."
The advocates of the market economy contest the conclusiveness of
this reasoning. They believe that p will lag so much behind P that d will
be smaller than the income which even those earning the lowest wages
get in the market society. There can be no doubt that this objection is
well founded. However, it is not based on praxeological considerations
and therefore lacks the apodictic and incontestable argumentative power
inherent in a praxeological demonstration. It is based on a judgment
of relevance, the quantitative appraisal of the difference between the

---

[6] The doctrine refuted in the text found its most brilliant expositor in John Stuart
Mill (*Principles of Political Economy* [People's ed. London, 1867], pp. 126 ff.). However,
Mill resorted to this doctrine merely in order to refute an objection raised against
socialism, viz., that, by eliminating the incentive provided by selfishness, it would
impair the productivity of labor. He was not so blind as to assert that the productivity of labor would multiply under socialism. For an analysis and refutation of Mill's
reasoning, cf. Mises, *Socialism*, pp. 173–181.

two magnitudes P and p. In the field of human action such quantitative cognition is obtained by understanding, with regard to which full agreement between men cannot be reached. Praxeology, economics, and catallactics are of no use for the settlement of such dissensions concerning quantitative issues.

The advocates of socialism could even go farther and say: "Granted that each individual will be worse off under socialism than even the poorest under capitalism. Yet we spurn the market economy in spite of the fact that it supplies everybody with more goods than socialism. We disapprove of capitalism on ethical grounds as an unfair and amoral system. We prefer socialism on grounds commonly called non-economic and put up with the fact that it impairs everybody's well-being."[7] It cannot be denied that this haughty indifference with regard to material well-being is a privilege reserved to ivory-tower intellectuals, secluded from reality, and to ascetic anchorites. What made socialism popular with the immense majority of its supporters was, on the contrary, the illusion that it would supply them with more amenities than capitalism. But however this may be, it is obvious that this type of prosocialist argumentation cannot be touched by the liberal reasoning concerning the productivity of labor.

If no other objections could be raised to the socialist plans than that socialism will lower the standard of living of all or at least of the immense majority, it would be impossible for praxeology to pronounce a final judgment. Men would have to decide the issue between capitalism and socialism on the ground of judgments of value and of judgments of relevance. They would have to choose between the two systems as they choose between many other things. No objective standard could be discovered which would make it possible to settle the dispute in a manner which allows no contradiction and must be accepted by every sane individual. The freedom of each man's choice and discretion would not be annihilated by inexorable necessity. However, the true state of

---

[7] This model of reasoning was mainly resorted to by some eminent champions of Christian socialism. The Marxians used to recommend socialism on the ground that it would multiply productivity and bring unprecedented material wealth to everybody. Only lately have they changed their tactics. They declare that the Russian worker is happier than the American worker in spite of the fact that his standard of living is much lower; the knowledge that he lives under a fair system compensates by far for all his material hardships.

affairs is entirely different. Man is not in a position to choose between these two systems. Human cooperation under the system of the social division of labor is possible only in the market economy. Socialism is not a realizable system of society's economic organization because it lacks any method of economic calculation. To deal with this fundamental problem is the task of the fifth part of this book.

The establishment of this truth does not amount to a depreciation of the conclusiveness and the convincing power of the antisocialist argument derived from the impairment of productivity to be expected from socialism. The weight of this objection raised to the socialist plans is so overwhelming that no judicious man could hesitate to choose capitalism. Yet this would still be a choice between alternative systems of society's economic organization, preference given to one system as against another. However, such is not the alternative. Socialism cannot be realized because it is beyond human power to establish it as a social system. The choice is between capitalism and chaos. A man who chooses between drinking a glass of milk and a glass of a solution of potassium cyanide does not choose between two beverages; he chooses between life and death. A society that chooses between capitalism and socialism does not choose between two social systems; it chooses between social cooperation and the disintegration of society. Socialism is not an alternative to capitalism; it is an alternative to any system under which men can live as *human* beings. To stress this point is the task of economics as it is the task of biology and chemistry to teach that potassium cyanide is not a nutriment but deadly poison.

The convincing power of the productivity argument is in fact so irresistible that the advocates of socialism were forced to abandon their old tactics and to resort to new methods. They are eager to divert attention from the productivity issue by throwing into relief the monopoly problem. All contemporary socialist manifestoes expatiate on monopoly power. Statesmen and professors try to outdo one another in depicting the evils of monopoly. Our age is called the age of monopoly capitalism. The foremost argument advanced today in favor of socialism is the reference to monopoly.

Now, it is true that the emergence of monopoly prices (not of monopoly as such without monopoly prices) creates a discrepancy between the interests of the monopolist and those of the consumers.

The monopolist does not employ the monopolized good according to the wishes of the consumers. As far as there are monopoly prices, the interests of the monopolists take precedence over those of the public and the democracy of the market is restricted, with regard to monopoly prices there is not harmony, but conflict of interests.

It is possible to contest these statements with regard to the monopoly prices received in the sale of articles under patents and copyrights. One may argue that in the absence of patent and copyright legislation these books, compositions, and technological innovations would never have come into existence. The public pays monopoly prices for things it would not have enjoyed at all under competitive prices. However, we may fairly disregard this issue. It has little to do with the great monopoly controversy of our day. When people deal with the evils of monopoly, they imply that there prevails within the unhampered market economy a general and inevitable tendency toward the substitution of monopoly prices for competitive prices. This is, they say, a characteristic mark of "mature" or "late" capitalism. Whatever conditions may have been in the earlier stages of capitalist evolution and whatever one may think about the validity of the classical economists' statements concerning the harmony of the rightly understood interests, today there is no longer any question of such a harmony.

As has been pointed out already,[8] there is no such tendency toward monopolization. It is a fact that with many commodities in many countries monopoly prices prevail, and moreover, some articles are sold at monopoly prices on the world market. However, almost all of these instances of monopoly prices are the outgrowth of government interference with business. They were not created by the interplay of the factors operating on a free market. They are not products of capitalism, but precisely of the endeavors to counteract the forces determining the height of the market prices. It is a distortion of fact to speak of monopoly capitalism. It would be more appropriate to speak of monopoly interventionism or of monopoly statism.

Those instances of monopoly prices which would appear also on a market not hampered and sabotaged by the interference of the various national governments and by conspiracies between groups

---

[8] Cf. above, p. 366.

of governments are of minor importance. They concern some raw materials the deposits of which are few and geographically concentrated, and local limited-space monopolies. However, it is a fact that in these cases monopolies. However, it is a fact that in these cases monopoly prices can be realized even in the absence of government policies aiming directly or indirectly at their establishment. It is necessary to realize that consumers' sovereignty is not perfect and that there are limits to the operation of the democratic process of the market. There is in some exceptional and rare cases of minor importance even on a market not hampered and sabotaged by government interference an antagonism between the interests of the owners of factors of production and those of the rest of the people. However, the existence of such antagonisms by no means impairs the concord of the interests of all people with regard to the preservation of the market economy. The market economy is the only system of society's economic organization that can function and really has been functioning. Socialism is unrealizable because of its inability to develop a method for economic calculation. Interventionism must result in a state of affairs which, from the point of view of its advocates, is less desirable than the conditions of the unhampered market economy which it aims to alter. In addition, it liquidates itself as soon as it is pushed beyond a narrow field of application.[9] Such being the case, the only social order that can preserve and further intensify the social division of labor is the market economy. All those who do not wish to disintegrate social cooperation and to return to the conditions of primitive barbarism are interested in the perpetuation of the market economy.

The classical economists' teachings concerning the harmony of the rightly understood interests were defective in so far as they failed to recognize the fact that the democratic process of the market is not perfect, because in some instances of minor importance, even in the unhampered market economy, monopoly prices may appear. But much more conspicuous was their failure to recognize that and why no socialist system can be considered as a system of society's economic organization. They based the doctrine of the harmony of interests upon the erroneous assumption that there are no exceptions to the rule that the owners of

---

[9] Cf. the sixth part of this book.

the means of production are forced by the market process to employ their property according to the wishes of the consumers. Today this theorem must be based on the knowledge that no economic calculation is feasible under socialism.